Gratitude
with
Dogs under Stars

New and Collected Poems

Debra Marquart

D1546177

North Dakota State University Press
Fargo, North Dakota

North Dakota State Univesity Press
Dept. 2576, PO Box 6050, Fargo, ND 581080-6050
www.ndsupress.org

Gratitude with Dogs under Stars
by Debra Marquart

LCCN: 2023942400
ISBN: 978-1-946163-60-8

Cover and Interior design by Nayt Rundquist
Cover image *Winter Moon* by Charles Beck. Image used by permission of the Beck family. Star photo by Free Nature Stock on Pexels, used under CC0 license.

The publication of *Gratitude with Dogs under Stars* is made possible by the generous support of the Muriel and Joseph Richardson Fund and other donors to the NDSU Press Fund and the NDSU Press Endowed Fund.

Kimberly Wallin, Director
Suzzanne Kelley, Publisher
Kyle Vanderburg, Assistant Acquisitions Editor
Mike Huynh, Graduate Assistant in Publishing
Nayt Rundquist, *Gratitude with Dogs under Stars* Project Manager

Printed in the United States of America

Names: Marquart, Debra K., author.
Title: Gratitude with dogs under stars : new and collected poems / Debra Marquart.
Description: First edition. | Fargo, North Dakota : North Dakota State University Press, [2023]
Identifiers: ISBN: 978-1-946163-60-8
Subjects: LCSH: Families--Poetry. | Love--Poetry. | Loss (Psychology)--Poetry. | Place (Philosophy)--Poetry. | Music--Poetry. | Nature--Poetry. | LCGFT: Poetry. | BISAC: POETRY / Women Authors. | POETRY / Subjects & Themes / Places. | POETRY / Subjects & Themes / Family. | POETRY / American / General.
Classification: LCC: PS3563.A7112 G73 2023 | DDC: 811/.54--dc23

Contents

New Poems | 2023

Small Buried Things | 2015

Greyhound Days

Our Gold and Yellow Making

This New Quiet

Everything's a Verb | 1995
Places Only the Body Knows

What do we say any more
to conjure the salt of our earth?
So much comes and is gone
that should be crystal and kept
    —Seamus Heaney "The Singer's House"

i made it up
here on this bridge between
starshine and clay
my one hand holding tight
my other hand
    —Lucille Clifton, "won't you celebrate with me"

New Poems | 2023

chokecherry

prunus melanocarpa

go in august with sisters
down the fly buzz dusty
rows of elms ashes poplars

that great grandfather planted
to slow the wind. go swinging
empty ice cream buckets braceleted

on wrists. all summer this ripening
sweaty cicada hum and
chokecherry's deadly green

drupes turned black cherry then
burnt umber. now the skin tough
and tart, leaves a sandy pucker

on the tongue, catch of grit
in the throat. our maroon fingers
thread branches as we heavy

the harvest into buckets—
the poison carried home
to cure cull, siphon

in colanders, steam-kitchen
then thicken to jams, syrups.
pint jars stored in root cellar rows,

the purple stain of summer
shored up against winter's long
white bleak. remember how

sometimes you'd swallow a pit,
sweet cyanide of childhood
preserved in bones.

Even on a Sunday Drive

it's possible to break your heart.
this smear on the freeway—a jumble
of checkered dark feathers against

a mottled white breast. impossible
to mistake the rufous brown,
the upturned spray of red tail feathers

edged with black. strange to see
the moment when the efficient killer
meets the greater death, the fatal blow

dealt by a speeding car just seconds
ahead. better to pity the mice, voles,
and rabbits, the snakes and warmbloods

who scuttle in short grass under
their swift talons. but the sight
of red-tailed hawks in winter,

perched in bare branches,
like frumpy winston churchills
officiating the freeway's cold ditches

in topcoat and tails, always makes
me laugh. but today the sight
of this smaller hawk, landed

in the emergency lane and turning
circles two miles up the road,
staring backwards with that look

on her face, *where is he?* reminds me
that hawks incubate their eggs
in cooperative pairs, mate for life,

and build nests like upturned bowls
of sticks to hold their young,
which makes me want to stop the car,

bend my forehead to the pavement
and whisper, *i'm sorry, i'm sorry,*
forgive me. but locked traffic

propels me forward and three miles
up the road another distraction—
a ryder truck encased in flames

parked across the median, the contents
blazing poker hot against the horizon.
already sirens approach in the distance

and three humans circle the catastrophe.

magnolia

nine blackened buds gathered on my desk   retrieved
by trespass into the blind southwest
corner of my neighbor's yard

where none of his windows faced magnolia's showings—
her first spring retreat from ice-dripped limbs,
catch of snow in sunlight, then

chill-pop of buds   finger-blossom feathering
of pink and white petals
preceding summer's green flourish.

and how I would sit on my deck in crisp air   surprised
by cool verbena, magnolia's champagne
of cupped blossoms.

she was my tree, in truth   trespasser of my fence
though in his yard planted
and whose foundation

he feared her roots threatened   too close to his corner
blind   did he know   what she was—
trespasser too quiet

in my delight, if I had leaned in   broadcast her beauty
over the fence   would he have
spared the axe.

stump of magnolia, now   this fall day in the blind corner
holes drilled in the trunk
to thwart further thriving.

nine blackened buds on my desk   vestiges fallen
magnolia's last blossoms
left to dry and blacken at the roots.

blind   did he know   what she was—
too quiet   in my delight
I blame myself   I blame myself.

When the First Love of the One You Love Dies

something in you goes silent, too.
didn't she lap up all the sweetness
with a hungry tongue, the hot fudge

sundaes he delivered to her
front porch swing, summer nights
after his first job folding men's shirts

at pomeroy's department store.
the billow of her teenage bedroom
curtains, what future love could compete

with those deep apostrophe
dimples. the two of them, so young,
her fingers clasping his arm

in the prom photo, his blue velvet
tux, the drape of her long white
formal covering the casts on her legs—

both broken that junior year
from shin splints running track.
their wide smiles at the absurdity,

the crutches angled against the wall
in the photo behind them. hard
to know what unsteadied her,

caused her to cast him off,
driftless and unloved into
the world, but you are grateful

for the course she set him on
toward you, dumb luck recipient
of love's sweet misfortune, a heart

improved through misery. who
did what to whom? does it matter
in the end, now death steps in

to sweep the equations. *I can still hear
her voice*, one friend said upon learning
of her end. that tongue so quick

and cruel, that made first marks
on the one you love, that tongue
so young that haunts each kiss

he now delivers to your willing lips.

—for Rosie

Landline

I kept the beige wall-mounted trimline telephone
with its lighted touchpad & Bell South label
hanging from its metal plate on my kitchen wall

long after I silenced the ringer & disposed of
the answering machine, long after I stopped
payment of the phone bill, long after discovering

that no dial tone droned on when I picked up
the receiver (I never picked up the receiver)
long after I learned that the cable carrying

the landline into the building no longer ran
into the building. But I kept the beige trimline
plugged into its metal plate on my kitchen wall

with its curling jump rope cord (which we girls
stretched thin into the bathroom, our umbilical
for private calls) because if the power went out

& all the plugged-in phones failed (because
the trimline was engineered to receive current
straight through the jack, a fact I learned

when our neighbor lady was struck by lightning
while gossiping during a thunderstorm)
so if the expected cataclysmic solar flare,

the really big one, finally hit earth
or the magnetic poles shift (as reported to do
every half a million years) knocking out all

cell phones & computers, not to mention
ATMs, bank accounts & cable TV
at least I could pick up the landline &

dial the number, that number that still
materializes on my tongue & say, hello
mother, hello, are you okay?

Come November

                        come
cold eye corrective, come pendulum
take wrecking ball to venerable walls

come cerulean wave, come
typhoon earthquake tsunami
blow the gentlemen from

utahiowasouthcarolinakentuckymaine
back to higher ground
or (better yet) homeward

to the distant shores
that spawned them   leave them
shipwrecked   washed up   jobless   uninsured

come classic EF5 tornado
good ol' midwestern tradition, come
barn-splintering wedge of gale force winds

come vacuum up this mess of a land
rip the flimsy scrim from the chambers
where black-robed justices

work their corrupted levers   these days

        it's tempting to curse biblical—
            to call down pestilence, plague, a pox upon
                both houses & the thundering hooves of horsemen—

instead, embrace november's wintry grip
        november come inevitable
            november come early & often   listen

can you hear that ticking
        like fingertips of sleet
            upon window panes—

it's the clicking of check-marks
    in ballot boxes
        the coming blizzard
          of millions.

—October 2018

What Hunts in These Woods

I do not understand how three raccoons
can climb into a garbage dumpster friends
then tumble out, spit-spat ash-can enemies.

My ears cannot detect a rabbit's foot thump
over the night-thick chorus of crickets, tree frogs,
cicadas, yet I know rabbits stomp their

furry soles to warn of predators. Still midnight
brings shrieks—if quick, a rabbit is taken;
if prolonged, a hawk is mating—and my dogs

go quiet in the bedding, whimper their old blood
knowing, which I may never know. Just as
they sense the musk of deer passing through

the woods below or the footfall of other dogs
by the jingle of tags. I've read that crows hold
funerals for their dead and memorize the faces

of those who've harmed them. Crows have
a distress call that sounds like *caw caw caw*
that does not mean *Help me, I'm in trouble,*

but instead means *Fly away, save yourselves,*
which suggests concern for community,
altruism. I don't know why cooper's hawks

kill other birds, but red-tailed hawks reserve
their talons for mice and voles, or why everybody
doesn't just break down and love the opossum,

who eats things humans detest, like deer ticks.
The opossum, whose females carry their young
in marsupial pouches or in a dozen-latched-row

along their spine. The opossum with its ratty tail
and pink nose, who risks losing its bare fingers
and opposable digits to frostbite, just like humans,

who are too often roadkill for their potbellied
crossings. Today, I surprised a raccoon
while depositing garbage in the dumpster.

He cowered in the corner when I lifted the cover.
Don't hurt me, his eyes said, *I'm just hungry*.
He didn't strike me as the enemy.

Winter Amaranth

Pulled from sleep I watch the dark outlines
of deer nuzzle soft ground beneath my spruce

and accept we will not have crocuses this spring
in the place where I knelt and nestled bulbs deep

in soil, fleshy corms encased in onion skin tunics,
ovaries turned up, adventitious roots pressed

down. All winter, I dreamt of their prayerful hands
royal purple and lavender, cresting cold ground.

We've lost so many this year, my dearest friend
among them, her fading a grievance I cannot

reconcile, this forfeiture that living on requires.
Spring will arrive, tulips trumpeting their orange

and red news. Daffodils will rise and spread
frilly white and yellow skirts. I don't begrudge

the deer who ate the bulbs, a tithe nature extracts.
Crocuses will grow in their bellies now, the stigmata

of saffron will crimson their blood just as
the heathered violet of my friend's voice

echoes in me like sweet amaranth, an undying
flower that blooms everlasting, and the deer

will be my family now.

—for Barbara Crow

a story from the eighties

that could never happen again
in that house on brookdale road
three blocks from the red river

where a pack of neighborhood girls
loved to ring my doorbell and sit
on my living room floor, pop pink

and blue bubblegum, paint
fingernails and toes in mauve
and purple sparkles and beg

to brush and braid my hair,
which was long and dark then
down to my waist, and I was young

and childless with plenty of time
they thought, to gossip about
barrettes and eye shadow and boys

as much as any ten-year-old knows
and organize sword fights in the kitchen
with the used-up paper tubes

from wrapping paper, and so
it was my door they ran to that day
when they spotted a painted turtle

wandering down the middle
of brookdale road like a toddler
on a tricycle festooned with red and blue

streamers for the neighborhood
fourth of july parade, and we all ran out
to admire his dark olive shell

and green-gold eyes, the striped
yellow neck he extended
to propel himself forward

carrying his house on his back
and the bright orange flashes
of his underside. he'd wandered

too far from the river, we guessed
and they fretted he'd get run over,
so I fetched a box and gloves

and scooped him up, then straight
into my plymouth fury along with
five or six ponytailed girls, all gum pops

and chatter in cutoffs and tank tops,
and we raced to gooseberry park,
no time for seat belts or sunglasses

or stopping to tell the parents.
imagine. on the shore of the red,
we set him down in the mud

near the swift brown current,
and nose in the air—no hesitation—
he descended the steep bank

and disappeared beneath
the ripples as we looked north,
the direction we knew the red flowed

then cheered when he bobbled
into view a few hundred feet
upriver, singing goodbye little turtle

goodbye. don't ever look back.

for a month that summer, remember

i taught at bowling green near mammoth caves and amassed enough books, bowls, wine glasses, and sun dresses, beyond the capacity of my two-door to return it all to michigan, so you drove down to help ferry home my surplus, and the absurd two-car tandem drive began, north on I-65 through louisville and indianapolis, passing all the important stops on your family's earlier migration, your father following a job with xerox, and you'd call me when we passed the exit to your old house, your old school, but we stayed on the highway, eager to get back to your house in Michigan. and sometimes you were out of sight, miles ahead, and sometimes just ahead, two car lengths, so I could make out the sheening slope of your silver acura. and sometimes I raced on, the naturally faster driver, the cherry red flash of my jetta, zooming by, four on the floor, or sometimes behind, like a comet trailing. and when we passed each other, we'd smile sideways when we lined up even in the two lanes, as if strangers or lovers on the way to some secret assignation. and when we hit I-69, we weren't above making the old joke, and we drove seven hours like this—bowling green to kalamazoo—as thousands passed us or fell behind, going north by fields and farms, indiana outskirts, where strangers in other cars exited, their journeys veering off, but we had no eyes for them, except around muncie when you called and said, careful, crazy driver in pickup speeding, or by fort wayne, traffic jam, and we made it home like this, traveling in tandem all these years together, intent on staying close.

—for Thomas Rice

Target

To get to housewares, electronics, sporting goods, you must first pass by girls' clothing. The tiny, flared skirts in pinks and yellows in the summer, deep blues and greens in the winter that stand between you and the things in the world you need to purchase.

All year, as you go to this store for greeting cards or new linens, you must first see the gauzy blouses with matching cotton shorts in summer, the frilly dresses in Easter egg colors. The crisp pleated back-to-school wool skirts in fall. In winter, the red velvet Santa dresses with white marabou ringing the sleeves and hemline wave to you.

And the ribbons! So delicate—tiny, silk bows stitched at the neckline or flowing in a wide swath from an empire waist. Easy then to imagine the fine hair that would need to be brushed, washed, pushed away from hot foreheads and braided, or pulled back into soft ponytails. You allow yourself this moment to forget the list of errands—what urgent thing is expected of you and where.

You can picture it all. The glowing nightlight and the stories that would have to be read again and again, until the words that came out of your mouth rushed out of hers, memorized from so much repetition. The duck-chatter of her voice. The sketches of houses and bright suns and stick figures she would draw at the kitchen table. The flannel pajamas with fishes or smiling half-moons or bear cubs on them.

You allow yourself this moment because you are safe among the bright lights and colorful packaging. And the list is right there in your hand, bold letters reminding you that you are only here to buy luggage.

Arrivals

First, catch the Blue Line to Charles De Gaulle, chat with the woman on the train in the seat next to you along nine stops in broken English about the time she visited New York during the dangerous-eighties and tell her about your husband who's traveling 4,153 miles from Chicago to Paris to meet you, tell her you imagine him

over the Atlantic in his little flying seat. Concentrate on keeping his plane in the air as the suburbs of Paris pass by—gray high rises, graffiti, garbage cans—more like the abandoned inner cities of the rust belt, not like the grand arrondissements you've rambled through these weeks, navigating cobblestone, your balcony

overlooking terra cotta rooftops, the chiming of church bells. Imagine. You ate unthinking in bistros, brasseries, admired terrines, foie gras, escargot, all the while thinking *this* was Paris. Recall now the story told to you by the stranger in the hotel about Napoleon III, how he stood in the Ille de la Cite in 1853 with Haussmann,

the civic planner, and said, *tear it all down*, an order that leveled the ancient core of Paris and allowed these wide boulevards to emerge, the modern city carved from the whole cloth of the medieval, like a garment with its loose seams turned inside out, its beauty hidden inside, the Paris available only to the wealthy or the fortunate few

and tourists like you and your husband, if he ever arrives, if you ever find the right terminal, gate where you will wait with limo drivers in wraparound sunglasses, black suits, holding placards bearing the names of strangers. Where you will wait behind velvet ropes with clusters of women and children holding flowers and balloons, all

breathless for the frosted glass doors marked *Arrivals* to slide open and reveal a face so beloved it causes arms to go up, voices calling, *here, here, here.* This endless wave of handsome roman noses, five o'clock shadows makes you wonder about your own handsome husband with a roman nose and a five o'clock shadow, wonder how you

met, what you saw in him all those years ago, wonder what's to stop you from grabbing another arm in this place of arrivals. They say Haussmann expropriated property from anyone who fell in the path of his renovations. He razed buildings, tore down statues with no sentiment just to make room for these spacious avenues.

Wow

my future mother-in-law
whispered from the backseat
the first time she witnessed

my parallel parking skills.
no herky-jerky motion, no
back and forth, just one

precise turn of the wheel,
a clean motion backward,
then tires lined up flush

with the the curb. she'd
transported a cooked turkey,
thanksgiving trimmings

and all, across three state lines
to meet me, her son's new
girlfriend. nothing left to chance

after his ex-wife accidentally
poisoned the family once
with a spoiled bird. back

from the mall now, our
black friday coupons used,
sweet potatoes and stuffing

warming in the oven. *what else
is this girl capable of,* she must have
wondered after whitnessing my expert

back up display into a tight,
impossible spot. turns out,
plenty.

and again it was summer

on the street between
the tattoo parlor and
the coffee shop, three

construction workers
break from jackhammers
under wood scaffolds

to smoke cigarettes
near the blue awning
of the copy store.

i pass through their time-
released cloud of sweat
and old spice, unshaven

faces and last night's
skin oil mix—caffeine,
nicotine, beer yeast,

and testosterone, Plus
cigarette smoke exhaled
into fresh air and traces

of sawdust buzzed clean
under sharp blades, a smell
almost mousey that always

signals summer and
i'm thirteen again
upstairs on the farm

in my short shorts
and kerchief halter
proud of my new tan

body, drawing back
gossamer bedroom
curtains glancing

below at construction
workers building our garage
in july's dead heat thinking

surely they must need
something to quench
their thirst, surely one more

tray of sweaty lemonade
glasses delivered
by my shaking hands.

Life with Repeaters Repeating

If I've said it once, I've said it a million times
people who are not listened to as children
are destined to repeat themselves as adults,
again and again, the same answers and questions.

People who are not listened to as children
will order you around, then double-check their orders.
Again and again, the same answers and questions,
the key, the lock, the garage door, the state of the freezer.

Will order you around, then double-check their order,
the grocery list, the dry cleaning, the errand after work,
the key, the lock, the garage door, the state of the freezer.
No rest for these offspring of careless listeners,

the grocery list, the dry cleaning, the errand after work.
Parents, preoccupied parents! Do us all a favor.
No rest for these offspring of careless listeners,
what the dog did, what your best friend said, what to make for dinner.

Parents, preoccupied parents! Do us all a favor
don't condemn us to a life with repeaters repeating,
what the dog did, what your best friend said, what to make for dinner.
Listen to them now, don't murmur *uh-huh*, and *sure*, and *what*.

Don't condemn us to a life with repeaters repeating
I'll declare it once again, twice, and thrice, if necessary,
listen to them now, don't murmur *uh-huh*, and *sure*, and *what*.
Even the loving ear is dulled to deafness by repetition

I'll declare it once again, twice, and thrice, if necessary,
destined to repeat ourselves as adults
even the loving ear is dulled to deafness by repetition,
if I've said it once, I've said it a million times.

Pre-Existing Conditions

I am my sister's keeper.
—Sister Simone Campbell, addressing the Assembly
of the Democratic National Convention, Sept. 5, 2012

Three weeks ago, my sister went on her lunch break
and turned right, for home, rather than left, for the clinic,

where she might have been forced to admit to the doctor
that the pain in her left arm was something more than

the chronic ache in her left shoulder from the ladder fall
while cleaning last year. Instead, she went home for soup,

which is where my brother found her the next morning,
seated at the kitchen counter with her head resting

in her arms, as if she'd only fallen asleep, after her boss
reported that she hadn't come to work. She rose

each day at 5 A.M to bake muffins and fresh bread,
to make the potato salad and rotisserie chickens

that stock the coolers and shelves for the convenience
of people who don't have time to cook. Too young

for Medicare, at 58, she earned an hourly wage
that held her just above the poverty line, just enough

to disqualify her for Medicaid. I see now how she fell
between the cracks. Sure, she tempted fate,

cooked with too many eggs, too much salt, sugar,
butter, and cream Food was the love she offered

the world, and didn't we gobble up every rich
thing she put before us? Did she calculate the cost

of the coverage offered her under the new health care act
and think, *Four hundred dollars a month. That's a car payment,*

that's forty hours of labor, a full week of wages. How I wish
she'd been forced to buy it. On that last morning,

did she turn right, for home, instead of left, for the clinic,
because she knew a trip to the doctor would mean

a quadruple by-pass, loss of a job, bankruptcy,
and the forced foreclosure of a house almost paid for.

(Seven hundred dollars left on the mortgage at the time
of her death.) So did she decide to take the pain

and risk it, believing she was too tough to die?
Well, she wasn't. To be human is to walk around

with pre-existing conditions—always some muscle
or valve poised to fail, some cell ready to grow wild.

Never before have I wanted to speak to my president
and say, please, hurry up with this. She was my sister,

do you understand? As children, we shared a bathtub,
in those years of once-a-week Saturday night washings.

I can still feel her soapy back against mine. As teenagers,
we shared a bedroom, whispering late into the darkness

between our twin beds, until one of us would grow tired
and say, *little red school house on the hill,* our private code

for "shut up now, so that I can get some sleep."

And Black Bear Said

Those small hands of yours barely move the air.
Let the swipe of my paw cut a swath for you.

We took to the cover of trees when brown bear
forced us from the open plains. We survived

the continent's ice sheet that took out Arctodus,
the short-faced one. Our generalist tastes sustain us,

huckleberries, hickory nuts, oak acorns, hazelnuts.
Arboreal omnivores, we've been known to raid

the caches of tree squirrels. That silver pendant
you're wearing of a grizzly—take it off.

We agree now to move inside you. Remember
we do our best work in-between times

crepuscular foraging at twilight and pre-dawn
when others are not hunting but dreaming.

Yes, we've mastered human tricks
undoing screw tops, opening door latches

but can you pull a cabinet from the wall
or dig out the heart of a tree to swab honey.

We can stand on the cold lip of a stream
and catch a trout in rainbow leap. Bobcats,

cougars may try to displace us. But we return
to our bone home without familiar markings.

If someone tries to harm you, we will paw
the ground and roar behind you. Those coyotes

that howl in the distance, *rup, rup, ra-ra-roooo*,
will remain in the distance.

What Pete Dexter Said

—South Dakota Festival of Books, September 25, 2010

This talk is supposed to be called Priming the Pump.
Now the way this usually goes, the less prepared I am

the better it turns out. If that's the case, today should be
very good. First off, remember, you are even

with everyone in the room. You've got a pencil
and paper. Forget about the book you just finished.

Clear the palate. Spit out what you've done
and start anew. (I would have prepared something

    for this talk but last year I got bit
    by a dog—a puppy who got too excited.

    The infection settled in my spine
    and spread. I was months in the hospital

    and worn down to nothing. I've been
    very sick, but I'm feeling better.)

Start over, and it's all in front of you. Once you begin
making choices, start cutting out what's possible;

deepen it; narrow your choices. You write a sentence
and you write it until you're really happy with it.

A page, a story, start to get a little pile of paper.
Something small and true, follow it

in that true way, wherever it goes.

Rotunda

This nation under God shall have a new birth of freedom
that government of the people, by the people, for the people,
shall not perish from the earth.
 —Lines from Abraham Lincoln's "Gettysburg Address" inscribed
 along rotunda, State Capital Building, Des Moines, Iowa

Under the pink super moon at perigee
last night as close to earth as it will come

the moon so large on the horizon
luminous peach floating in the sky

reminded me of the time as a child
on a car trip, when the moon loomed

so bright through the car's rear window
that I warned my parents we were being

followed. *The moon is not chasing you.*
But this week's pink supermoon

did not look like the moon at all.
For one night she was Theia again,

the planet experts believe collided
with proto earth 4.5 billion years ago

then splintered off to become this fragment
we know as the moon, a dead rock

distant and exiled from us, caught up
in earth's orbit. And looking at it

I wondered how something that represents
an event of such unspeakable violence

could now be so unspeakably beautiful.
Just as under this rotunda, lofty

dome that looks up, like an intricate
camera's lens toward the celestial,

and under whose eye the powerful work,
makes me wonder if we will ever be able to see

as the rotunda sees, the long curving arc
of time, to aspire to its challenge

of greatness, to teach us to cauterize
the terrible injustices around us,

to help us stop the bleeding,
to turn wounds into scars.

This year, when the world stopped,
was our year of looking in and

looking up. Can we learn? Can we find
the light to navigate this awful passage?

Can we aspire toward a place after violence—
that hard-won place of awe-filled beauty.

Gratitude with Dogs under Stars

bless this night   bless
    the small bladders of dogs
        urgent under moonlight

bless raccoon and her brothers
    those masked three a.m. bandits
        who lowered themselves

on branches of viburnum
    with eerie five-fingered hands
        into the dumpster   who scavenged

melon rinds   burger wrappers
    tossed oily tuna cans to pavement
        with a chime that pricked the ears

of my sleeping lhasas   these litter mates
    bred to guard monasteries
        who have warned me awake

bless their low ruff and whine
    and even bless the scramble
        for boots coats leashes   propelled

into this obsidian night   under indigo skies
    crisp exhale puffed into clouds.
        above us   velvety stillness   sirius

a twinkling beacon
    in a stippled southern sky
        castor and pollux   those star twins

throwing geminid tracers—
    scattershot pin pricks of radiance into darkness
        above us, this afterimage

of ancient supernovas—billions of years old—
    violent light moving toward us
        let us witness   their brilliance going

from this blessed place on earth
    we fortunate mortals on the ground
        living amongst terrestrials

who sniff and paw the dirt
    who kick back their legs
        and growl at the darkness

while above us—
    so much deadly light
        to wish upon

all spring sunny afternoon

i play guitar   i play guitar
and sing to creek facing windows
i play guitar and sing

to creek facing windows
as hawks flex and reel
high in the thermals

four foot wingspans
black pantagium fan of feathers
spread and turn   spread

and turn   i sing
and play guitar   as hawks glide
above the treeline

as two rabbits
chase through underbrush
hop over hopscotch

pivot   leapfrog   then circle
as finches   fat robins   cardinals
flit branch to branch

launch wide arcs across the yard
from tree to feeder to deck
then quick drop

to grass   to hop   to peck
as fat squirrels creep out
risk the lawn

whisker-flick-right   whisker-flick-left
long tail shake   then full-on-roll
back-scratch exposure

of bright copper underbellies
are we shedding long winter
are we trying on our new spring bodies

all spring sunny afternoon
i play guitar   i play guitar
and sing to creek facing

windows   as dusk comes on
as glass panes reflect
my face   I see

what I've been watching
is it joy is it
joy is it

Small Buried Things | 2015

For Tom, Adam, and Gabe

Things Not to Put in Your Mouth

—Medical Display, Iowa State Historical Museum, Des Moines, Iowa

a penny   a quarter   a button   a paperclip
    safety pins, closed and open
        most ingested while changing diapers

In two shadow boxes, Dr. James Downing displayed the objects
    he'd extracted from patients' food and air passages
        between 1929 and 1956.

a wishbone   a kernel of corn (overlarge)   a pen nib
    beads from a necklace with the string still attached
        a nail   a screw   a cover from a bottle of Anacin

Thumbtacked in rows, suspended in glassine envelopes
    the objects floated in glass cases, a warning
        about things not to put in your mouth.

a toothpick   a rhinestone earring   a wadded up ball of paper
    a metal snap   a cocklebur seed, spikey as a porcupine
        a long sewing needle   a sardine can turnkey

many small chicken bones   things with sharp edges
    cumbersome things that get caught in the throat
        things that go down hard and refuse to come up

a Daughters of the American Revolution pendant
    a gold hinge from a jewelry box   a price tag marked .89 cents
        for Item #1025293 from the Younkers Department Store

The exhibit includes the doctor's leather medical bag
    and his instruments of extraction   a tracheal dilator
        a uvula dilator   laryngeal and esophageal forceps

along with a humorous note, jotted in a hospital report,
    feed her anything but nickels and pennies, the note reads,
        beside the very nickel extracted from the child's throat.

Greyhound Days

Kablooey Is the Sound You'll Hear

then plaster falling and the billow of gypsum
after your sister blows a hole in the ceiling
of your brother's bedroom with the shotgun
he left loaded and still resting on his dresser.

It's Saturday, and the men are in the fields.
You and your sister are cleaning house
with your mother. Maybe your sister hates
cleaning that much, or maybe she's just

that thorough, but somehow she has lifted
the gun to dust it or dust under it (you are busy
mopping the stairs) and from the top landing
where you stand, you turn toward the sound

to see your sister cradling the smoking shotgun
in her surprised arms, like a beauty queen
clutching a bouquet of long-stemmed roses
after being pronounced the official winner.

Then the smell of burnt gunpowder
reaches you, dirty orange and sulfurous,
like spent fireworks, and through the veil
of smoke you see a hole smoldering

above her head, a halo of perforations
in the ceiling—the drywall blown clean
through insulation to naked joists, that dark
constellation where the buckshot spread.

The look on your sister's face is pure
shitfaced shock. You'd like to stop and
photograph it for blackmail or future
family stories but now you must focus

on the face of your mother, frozen there
at the base of the stairs where she has rushed
from vacuuming or waxing, her frantic eyes
searching your face for some clue about

the extent of the catastrophe. But it's like
that heavy quicksand dream where
you can't move or speak, so your mother
scrambles up the steps on all fours,

rushes past you, to the room where
your sister has just now found her voice,
already screaming her story—*it just went off!
it just went off!*—as if a shotgun left to rest

on safety would rise and fire itself.
All this will be hashed and re-hashed around
the supper table, but what stays with you
all these years later, what you cannot forget,

is that moment when your mother
waited at the bottom of the steps
for a word from you, one word,
and all you could offer her was silence.

Never Mind

Lately, I've been forgetting the words for things.
Tortilla, for example, in the Mexican restaurant
I am helpless. *A type of flatbread, made from wheat*

or corn, I might offer description in the absence
of the word or shout, *What is the casing
in which a burrito is wrapped*, as if this were *Jeopardy!*

Lately, too, I've been phoning myself, surprised
to see my own name light up on the LED
when the landline part of me must dial the cell

self, lost in the tangle of sheets or left behind
a stack of books still mulling over something
I read by Pessoa. Never mind. My brain

cleans out its closets each night, discards words
and phrases like garments that are old-fashioned,
ill-fitting, or haven't been off their hangers in years.

"Can you help me out," my student says.
"What's the name of that tragic jazz singer?"
(She thinks I'll know this because I'm old.)

Voice like Chinese porcelain, gardenia behind
the ear. We puzzle over it for minutes
before I google, "lady sings the blues."

And then there's the strange case of my friend
the botanist, who can reel off the Latin name
of any plant—castor bean (*ricinus communis*),

black cohosh (*cimicifuga racemosa*), mugwort
(*artemisia vulgaris*)—but who could not remember
the title of a film or the actors who starred in it

if you tied her down and beat the bottoms
of her feet. "Lover Boy," is how she refers
to every movie star. "You know, the one

who was married to that Cutie-Pie." Surely,
this is medical. I must request the Latin name
for the remedy, or stop by the apothecary,

or just break down and visit my physician—
good old what's-her-name—and confess all.
Never mind. The phone is sure to ring someday

from the endless bottom of my purse.
The message, when I manage to retrieve it,
will be long and full of unrecognizable jargon.

The voice of the nurse, no doubt, with all the gory details.

Greyhound Days

Because your mother is the Typhoid Mary
of travel. Because lightning, blizzards, locusts,
plague her travel days. Because that one time

in Minneapolis, some pilot-error, failing
engine part, or threat of nuclear disaster
necessitated an overnight stay, she now refuses

to fly. Too often, she will recount that airline-
stranded night for you—the cold shuttle ride
to the hotel, no PJs, toothbrush, or clean undies,

where all night she watched the green hinge
click of digits until the three a.m. wake-up call.
Besides, she says, why start out in Bismarck

going westbound for Bozeman by catching
an eastbound flight to Minneapolis?
So it's Greyhound days for her, and for you,

this day after Christmas, it's the drop-off drive
to the truck stop on the unlit edge of town,
where you'll stamp your feet, puff your cheeks

in the snowy dark, waiting for the Greyhound
with the goth girls and the tattooed boys,
with the gaunt-cheeked, luggage-less

chain smoker, and that one young mother
who's been criss-crossing the country
with her two toddlers and a colicky baby

since your own Greyhound days. You realize
at the approaching purr of the diesel engine,
at the grinding downshift of gears and the chirp

of airbrakes braking. Before the door folds
unfolding and passengers begin to disembark,
you realize you do not want to let your mother

go alone into this high northern night
through mountain passes, frozen wheat fields,
past oil rigs pumping their thin elbows

in the dark. But she grabs the nearest
passenger, the scruffy-bearded, nose-pierced
boy with hair dyed jet-black, just like yours

was in the eighties and begins to drill him—
Is it warm on the bus? Are there seats available?
Is the driver nice?—which, he answers

to your amazement, tossing his smoke
to the sidewalk in a splash of sparks,
making you realize your mother

would be an excellent person to have along
at a rock concert or the holocaust or any
huge natural disaster, this survivor,

who grabs her floral bag to board the steps
not looking back, as you watch her
through smoky glass, moving down the aisle,

checking each seat row-by-row, with those eyes
that always saw everything, until she chooses
the best one, left side, one row behind the driver,

and stashes her bag, never once glancing down
at you, below in the cold, waving *goodbye,*
be careful, waving *safe travels,* waving *love you.*

Even as the driver downshifts, your mother
leans forward to chat—dark silhouette of her hand
on the headrest—even as he undoes the brake,

turns off the interior light and the bus jerks
to a start, you realize you are still waving, waving,
waving at the darkness now, waving at the spot

where you imagine she must be sitting.

Couples Traveling

Worse than traveling alone is to be stranded in security
behind couples, especially old traveling couples, now jacket

and vestless as they fuss shoeless in stocking feet, turn belts,
wallets in their hands as if newly-invented things. Torture

to wait by the conveyor, watch the wife pair and unpair
their shoes, zip and unzip her carry-on, which *she* wanted

to check, but, *no*, he refused. Almost to enter the dust
of their bedroom, to stand invisible on the plush carpet

by the bedside where they read by lamplight, discuss bosses,
bills and children, all grown now, like the daughter who delivered

the grandkids they are now going to visit or the son who drove them
to the airport at early light. Even as the husband enters

the metal detector, you know his pockets are full of loose coins
and chewing-gum aluminum, just as the wife's suitcase contains

liquids too large and numerous for the baggies. What to do
but return them again and again through the X-ray, followed by

pat downs and manual searches. You'll hear all about this later
when you find them occupying the seats next to you on the plane

where the husband will grab the male end of his seat belt
and attempt to slot it into your female strap, where a cell phone

will ring, loud and buried deep in the folds of their carry-on,
even as the plane taxis the runway, even as the wife digs deep

and answers, *yes, dear, we're on the plane*, even as the husband smiles
and takes full command of your rightful half of the armrest.

Traveling with Guitar

For you can travel with a screaming red rolling bag
and float unnoticed on conveyors, through terminals

or you can lug half a moose rack from Maine
to Minnesota, carry it like a broken wing through airports

as my friend Gro did, and draw only the curious touches
of children waiting at gates. But dare to travel with a guitar

and invite confessions from strangers in pinstripe suits
of garage band summers, invite winks, *gotcha* smiles,

and devil's horns *rock-on* gestures. Invite finger natches,
long tongue licks, and the rubberneck backward glances

to check if you are someone famous. To dare to travel
with a guitar is to mark yourself charismatic megafauna

of the airport terminal. Old friend, what else could I do
but carry you? I have stored you in closets, propped you

in corners, hunched over you late-nights, staring perplexed
at the mysteries of your neck. Body of my body, string

of my strings, see how the whole world began to hum and sing
that day at thirteen when I opened the big birthday box.

Door-to-Door

Within minutes we were in the bedroom.
    I know this sounds bad.
Worse still to admit I'd said, *sure,*
    come on over, when the man
called to inform me I was the lucky winner
    of a ten-piece set of cutlery.

So the stranger with sharp knives arrived
    in a green plaid polyester blazer
carrying a silver Kirby vacuum cleaner
    and a suitcase full of accessories
including this clear Petrie dish-like attachment
    lined with a cotton wafer, thin as a host,

that connected to the vacuum's hose
    to demonstrate, in one quick stroke
all the dust mites and dried skin cells
    the salesman could extract
from my curtains, couch, and mattress.
    Which is how we ended up

on our hands and knees in the bedroom
    with him asking, *do you really want to live
in this filth?* And me answering, *well, yes,*
    because I didn't have eight hundred dollars
or whatever ridiculous amount of money
    a Kirby cost in 1983. I'll admit

I feigned interest to justify accepting
    the cutlery, then I hedged to get him
out the door, which he read as my willingness
    to negotiate, saying, *ho, ho, lady,
you sure drive a hard bargain,* leading to
    a succession of calls to his manager

waiting in some supervisor underworld,
    whom he harangued over my tan,
wall-mounted princess telephone, negotiating
    this once-in-a-lifetime, heretofore-unseen

bargain-basement price with such ruthless persuasion
    it required the manager to hang up

and consult his own fictitious supervisor.
    As the phone shrilled off my kitchen wall—
offer following counter-offer—my brutish boyfriend
    was finally raised from the basement
where he was practicing guitar
    or masturbating or sneaking in calls

to his next girlfriend. And at first sight
    of my boyfriend's black Irish eyes
the salesman gulped and exited with the Kirby
    and his suitcase of accessories
recognizing in those eyes a brand of mean
    it would take me years to identify.

So maybe I did fill out a simple form
    offering my name, address,
and phone number for the lucky chance
    to win a membership at a local gym
or a cherry red Corvette or whatever
    worthless thing I desired

enough to slip all of my information
    into a plexiglass box at the mall.
These days I don't answer a door or a call
    unless I know exactly who lurks
for me on the other side of the wall.
    I think about that Kirby sometimes

wonder how it might have improved
    my situation. Mostly, I hope nobody
is forced to sell shit door-to-door
    in these inhospitable times. Even when
the salesman returned three days later
    to retrieve the green plaid polyester blazer

he'd left behind (on purpose or in haste
        I'll never know) I'll admit I was short
with him. Even after he fished the polaroid
        from his pocket to show me his kids—
a toddler and an infant in highchairs,
        chubby faces smeared red

with spaghetti-o's—even then
        I was not moved to buy the machine.
The princess phone is in a landfill somewhere
        returned to the elements by now
and the boyfriend, well,
        he got what he deserved.

A Kirby is a good investment, I still maintain
        if you have that kind of disposable income.
But the knives in the end proved worthless.
        The handles, cheaply made
and the blades never sharp enough
        when it finally came time to use them.

Balance

i.

Too careful, that first day, we sat on the floor palm-to-palm making church steeples. He showed me the trick where two can lean back-to-back in mid-air and rest easy, if one does not press harder than the other.

ii.

Leaving his building that afternoon, I saw a full moon rise in the east, a cool blue wafer, like an offering in the sky; and the sun, an exhausted swimmer, disappeared into the orange pool of the west. I thought, if only I could reach up and cup both of them in my palms, I would feel certain.

iii.

Today he comes in happy with some things from his apartment, things we can use—a cheese grater, a spatula, a red soup ladle. He pulls the utensils from the box and turns them in the air, one-by-one like a magician—a potato peeler, a pancake turner—before placing them in the drawer by the stove. I sit on the floor keeping track, I realize, for the day when I will again have to separate them from my own.

Ecdysis

The female lobster waits by the den
of the largest male, wafts perfume
in his direction, the invitation to mate

or be eaten. Boxing proceeds until
she rests her pincers on his head,
a sign of her readiness. Only she

knows when to secrete the enzyme
that exuviates her shell, splits it open
like a too-small suit, to slough off

the old carapace, a process named
after the Greek, *ekdysis*, meaning
"getting out." What happens next

in the watery room, no one likes to
talk about—except to marvel how
it's worked for 500 million years—

but I've read that she surrenders
her soft parts to him, then rests
under his protection for weeks

turning in milky strands of softness
until her hard shell returns, the chitin
of armor growing back like a tunic.

That they rise to part without
a backward glance is only human
whimsy to report. From birth,

lobsters know to escape
the outgrown by tattooing
a replica of the exoskeleton

onto soft tissue. Tracing each follicle
and mandible, every section of spine
and pigment like a blueprint,

they withdraw blood from claws,
calcium from the spent shell.
Storing resources in gastroliths

along stomach walls, they wait
in murky depths for the imperceptible
sign to drink saltwater, enough to swell

the body, force off the old cage.
How difficult, this reverse birth,
threading the meat of claws backwards

through collapsed narrow joints,
then floating away from the shipwreck
with new antennae, new gills, mouth, and eyes.

Lazer Land Outing with Boys

I'm not the boys' mother, although the picture
of us so convinces the arcade manager
that he shouts, *Happy Mother's Day,*

the moment we storm the entrance,
escaping the rain—these two blond boys,
their dark-haired father, and me, the female

free radical who's become attached
to this all-male atom. Quirks of custody
result in the boys spending Mother's Day

with their father, and Father's Day
with their mother, who is presently
in Chicago having lunch or skiing

in the Sierra Nevada or possibly
snorkeling off the coast of Bermuda.
Pot roasts are simmering somewhere

but not in our kitchens. *Decided to
take Mom out on her special day?*
The arcade manager persists.

I should correct him in his error. Truth is,
the weather's been bad, television
worse, church is out of the question,

and short of killing each other
we've elected this morning to hurl
basketballs through electronic hoops,

grip careening wheels of arcade race cars,
our feet heavy on the accelerators
as we pass through movie landscapes

where we will lose the road, spin out,
roll over and walk away unscathed.
Now, it's time for the heavy artillery—

flak jackets with velcro straps, combat
helmets, power packs, and lazer pistols
with hair-sensitive triggers in our palms.

Do we want teams, the attendant
asks us, *or every man for himself?*
We look at the boys. Teams, they nod,

the big people against the little.
The attendant powers up the computer,
a small whine rising from its belly

spreads through our power packs
and pistols, our chests and torsos
light up our fluorescent patches—

marking the targets on our bodies
worth hitting, the tender spots
only those we love can see. *Be good*

to Mom now, the attendant says,
still misunderstanding. We enter
the dark cave of the shooting gallery,

where we will lie in wait behind
barriers, roll, tumble, and dodge.
Where we will lurk on one knee

and search the dark,
then take aim at each other,
as only family can.

What I Learned from Playing Hearts

Nothing counts until the first heart is broken,
although the queen of spades can do damage anytime.
No one's likely to get hurt on the first move,
so if you have a profusion of spades, keep her near.

Although the queen of spades can do damage anytime,
better to hold trouble close, rather than wonder,
so if you have a profusion of spades, keep her near.
Remember, diamonds and clubs count for nothing—

better to hold trouble close, rather than wonder.
Begin by exhausting your weakest suit,
remember, diamonds and clubs count for nothing,
and try pawning off your hearts on others.

Begin by exhausting your weakest suit,
watch for people who keep changing the subject,
and try pawning off your hearts on others.
Beware of players who attempt to do the same to you.

Watch for people who keep changing the subject,
although evasion only works for so long.
Beware of players who attempt to do the same to you:
eventually someone's got to pay for the queen.

Although evasion only works for so long,
sometimes it's good to have an abundance of trouble:
eventually someone's got to pay for the queen;
and if you're in too deep, you can try to shoot the moon.

Sometimes it's good to have an abundance of trouble:
no one's likely to get hurt on the first move,
and if you're in too deep, you can try to shoot the moon.
Nothing counts until the first heart is broken.

Ground Oregano

Bitter green, bottled dust of pungent woods
I've carried across cities and states, past its prime,

almost gone now, *origanum vulgare*. Twenty-five years
since I tucked it deep in the spice rack after he insisted

he was allergic, although I'd used it in the lasagna,
chili, and spaghetti he'd eaten without illness

or complaint, so I guessed he was lying to make
a fuss, just as he invented a problem with dust

that required me to do the cleaning, and a fear
of mechanics and shopkeepers that made groceries,

and oil changes my job. Just as he interrupted
every story I told with words like *ostensibly*

and *presumably* because he was a spoiled first son
of a fussy mother who interviewed every teacher,

every piano and guitar tutor she hired as if he were heir
to the throne of Antigua. Eventually, I pinched

the bitter green into everything, then fled with the vial,
filed all these years behind my cinnamon, thyme,

and cumin. Even now, I see it on the back shelf,
unusable, almost spent, *Oros ganos*, from the Greek,

meaning, *joy on the mountain*. When fresh and strong
oregano can numb the tongue, make difficult words

unsayable. What have I neglected to mention?
His mother was his first grade teacher. Each day

they'd walk to school carrying matching briefcases.
After school, they sat together at the kitchen table.

While she prepared lesson plans, he busied himself
marking in red the erroneous papers of his classmates.

Scent

That Christmas Eve
we watched Mother open present
after present, useful socks, a colorful blouse, cotton pajamas,

waited for the jeweled bottle
to rise from its wrapping, for the *ooh*s
and *aah*s and *you shouldn't have*s. Fragrance of juniper, sage,

narcissus. Through frosted
drug store windows, two weeks earlier,
we'd spied Father turning amber bottles in the air, watched him

hand money to the lady
behind the counter. We'd felt smug
knowing what Mother was getting, she who kept our gifts

hidden in the cedar chest
under the airtight box with her tulle veil,
crushed rose bouquet, and ivory dress with its row of satin buttons.

What happened
to the extravagant gift, my sister and I
must have wondered, then neglected to ask, then forgot we ever knew.

Perfume disperses in layers,
over time. Hint of mandarin, lavender,
sandalwood. The top note is volatile and brilliant, a whiff of citrus,

quick to meet the nose
then evaporate. The heart note
is often flowery, the familiar body of the scent, a whisper of hyacinth

or violet. The base note contains
the heaviest molecules, ongoing and slow
to develop, begging the questions of musk and earth.

Thugs

Rather than write the memo
about the troubling colleague
I go out to weed the flowerbed,
beat back the carpet of quack grass
that's overgrown its boundary,
search under the green and red
explosion of roses, behind blue spires
of delphinium for the surreptitious
sprigs of pink evening primrose
that I formally removed from this bed
seasons ago, after I discovered
it gossiped about the blazing star,
overran the coreopsis, choked back
the dianthus. The mother plant
has been compost years now,
still her opportunistic runners
thread beneath the surface, spread
tendrils, blossoms, seeds. Beware
the blushing flower you invite into
your midst. Just like the sweet mint
I once thought it lovely to include
in the pot of basil, thyme, oregano,
rosemary, until it choked back
anything else green. Some things
must control every academic inch.
Thugs, they're called, garden thugs.
Too late before I realized
how she worked against me,
threw adventitious shoots,
spread stalks in the dark,
even in deadly silent winter
even while all around me
pretended to sleep.

Some Things about That Day

The placards I walked through. Wet raincoat on a hook. Questionnaire on a clipboard placed before me. Couples sat around me in the waiting room. They were young. What am I saying? I was only thirty-two.

But I remember, the men seemed the more bereft. Facing forward, their elbows resting on knees, their faces covered with hands. Or pushed back hard in the seats, gazing at a spot on the floor, legs stretched out in the aisles.

Difficult to remember the order in which things happened. The clipboard taken away, my name was called—our names were all called, the waiting room emptying and filling. Small orange pill in a tiny plastic cup. Water for washing it down. I was led to another room.

The gown that tied at the back, the bright fluorescent light, the posters with diagrams on the walls. Plenty of time to look around. The sound of vacuuming in another room.

The doctor arrives, hurried and unfriendly. Her one day in this clinic, she's flown in from another state. Death threats follow her. She asks me if I want to proceed. I tell her, *yes.* I lie back in the stirrups. The apparatus arrives—a silver canister on wheels with gauges and hoses attached to a long, cylindrical tube, thin like a spout. The sound of vacuuming close now. The nurse by my side, holding my shoulder. The doctor working away behind the thin film of my gown.

A blank space surrounds this moment. Sleepy from the sedative, yes, and numb. But let me not gloss over it. A feeling of tugging, mild discomfort. When the vacuum stops, the doctor asks if I want to know the sex. I tell her, *no.*

When I informed my husband I was pregnant, he said, *Is it mine?* Not the best beginning. We'd been married a month. Married on Leap Day. Who else's could it be? He had an important meeting at work that day, some critical task. I had driven myself.

Sleep, after the procedure. (My friend tried to soften it for me afterwards. *Just say you had a procedure, dear.*) Nothing about it was procedural. I woke in a room of sleeping beauties. Afterwards, cramping, nausea. Faint, when I woke up, dizzy.

Orange juice and back down for twenty minutes. And then the odd assemblage of street clothes smoothed onto my limbs, the parting advice from the nurse, the script for a prescription pushed into my hand. Strange to walk out the door. The protesters gone. My car started just fine, slipped right into gear. I backed out, went forward. Drove light-headed to the drug store.

At the pharmacy, the man in the white coat looked at me when I handed him the script. Could he see from the prescription where I'd been? A softness dawned on his face. *Go home*, he said. They would deliver it.

Only then, in the car, did I start to cry. So stupid. Over the kindness of the pharmacist. When I got home, my husband was on the couch, watching the NBA playoffs. Even before the drugs arrived—even after—he couldn't stop telling me what a brave girl I had been.

Warrior

So this student whose haircut makes him look like a sharp
fraternity man, this student with a hatchet nose and eyes

like a watchful eagle, really, even in poetry class, who wears
a volleyball uniform to school because practice immediately

follows prosody, who writes poems about patrols and dust offs
and how his wife won't listen as they lie in bed after making love,

and I, too, have not been listening closely enough to this student
who writes poems about the shrapnel embedded in his right thigh

and scars and things he had to do in the dirt and heat. And still
I am blind and thinking these are such good historical poems,

persona poems, really good World War II poems, until I see
words like *collateral damage*, until I see IEDs and desert imagery,

not jungle imagery, then I realize, no, I have been mistaken,
this is not Vietnam, not the South Pacific, this is the next generation

of warriors we have sent to do our work, groomed to come back
wounded, guilty, dead, silent or full of stories that no one is willing

to sit still long enough to listen to, or hear told—not this well or truly.

Nil Ductility

Time now to wonder about Bruce who sold
laminated timber beams out of his Fargo office,
the old growth forested in Oregon and East Glacier,

then planed, bent, glued, and shipped cross-country
from Montana in semis. The Douglas fir arches
and load-bearing trusses that supported the canopies

and curved interiors of tall churches, office buildings,
and shopping malls—all the gracious spaces where hallowed
work is done. Winter afternoons in the eighties I'd sluice

from campus through the snow in my Fury to his office,
Building Supplies, Inc., and sit in the second desk,
across the room, as Bruce took complaints, argued

with architects, calculated lineal feet. I'd type, file,
read my schoolbooks when my inbox was empty,
then talk across the room after all the estimates

were faxed. It was Bruce who taught me about nil ductility
after my Fury broke down in twenty-below zero,
explaining how even steel has its limits, in extremes,

becomes brittle and shatters, rather than bending
or deforming as it would in normal temperatures.
Even then, Bruce was going blind from MS,

from exposure to chemicals during his tours
with the 79th Combat Engineers. Even then,
sometimes he'd call me over to read the fine print,

and sometimes at the end of the day, he'd pull open
his bottom drawer, remove the pack of photographs,
some faded color, some black-and-white, all frayed

and graying at the edges, ringed with a rubber band
which he'd remove with careful fingers, then hand
to me, one image at a time, describing the concussion

of the blown bunker, the green sandbags raining
down, how the white femur and tibia of his friend
shattered like fractured timber from a land mine.

The photos were contraband, he explained,
yet all the GIs took them, smuggled the film
out of country to be developed, then stored

for safekeeping after the war. By the eighties
the photos must have been stashed in lockboxes
and offices across the country, so wives and children

of vets would not find them. How many times
did he hand me the glossy smile of his younger self
on leave in Da Nang, beer in hand, arm thrown over

a buddy, ready to ship for R & R in Singapore.
How many times did I hold in my hands
the flat profile of the Vietcong—the open eyes

and the swollen lips of the boy who attacked
their camp that night, whose skin was bruised gray
and buzzing with flies by morning, whose body

lay on the periphery in mud until first light made it safe
for the GIs to come out and discover the identity
of their attacker. Rare to see the enemy, he said,

so they were amazed to roll him over and find
this boy—his body so thin, his small hands,
his young face, all they could do was circle him

and take these photographs, like the one we held
in our hands. I looked, because I thought I should.
I listened because he needed me to, still bearing

all that weight so many years later, the pressure
reducing him, I could see, even as we sat together
in the dwindling light at Building Supplies, Inc.

Ground Zero

Small Buried Things

I.   Silos

ground zero   we believed
    we were   ground zero
        north dakota, 1964

minute men sleeping in silos   by the thousands
we knew   we couldn't say   we didn't know

ICBMs pockmarking the landscape
encased in concrete silos   six stories deep
buried in pastures
surrounded by cyclone wire
where holsteins muzzled through
for ungrazed grass

silos   bordering wheatfields
where farmers passed close by
with plows   seeders   combines
watched by soldiers
year round   in uniform   rifles in hand

small buried things   the great mirror underworld
grain silos above   missile silos below

    some people said they felt safer
    some said it helped the local economy
    some liked the men the missiles brought to town

and there were launch command centers
disguised as family ranch houses
sprinkled around the countryside

    the basketball hoop above the garage door
    the radio tower on the roof
    the army jeep parked in the drive
    the chain-link fence around the perimeter

and below ground   deep concrete bunkers
where launch sequences were memorized
by the buried few   the survivors
        those who would avenge us
        at the ready   to strike   after we were obliterated

for decades   they memorized codes   protocols   launch sequences
        controlling the cluster of ten missiles each at their command

we knew   we couldn't say   we didn't know

but look around you   to the west   minot air force base
        to the east   grand forks air force base
                how many air bases does one state need?

only the best get stationed up north, the airmen said
        what else could they say about drawing the short straw
                the assignment in siberia   surely
                        they'd offended someone as powerful as stalin
                                to be shipped here

strategically located   we were told
we were strategic   russia

not as far away as it might seem
one quick arc over the ice cap
north dakota to moscow

the shortest line between two points   they told us
        the small converging world
                of the arctic circle

we knew   we couldn't say   we didn't know

ground zero   years later   we learned
        north dakota would have been the third largest
                nuclear power in the world

if we'd seceded from the union

II.   Chill Factor

sometimes at parties in moorhead
my friend's late night rambling
hushed   as if fearing microphones
in the walls   crazy talk, really
about what was buried
in the countryside   up north

everyone gone from the party   just a few of us
slumped deep in couches
blowing smoke rings
the night's music playing   on repeat

the cup from the keg's last beer
warm in our hands   my friend would begin
the story   again   it never varied
about his late night drive
        up north   years ago   three a.m.
                twenty below   outside, the chilblain night
                        the darkened eyelids of farmhouses

inside the car   the radio playing soft rock, he said
the DJ's distant voice   the heater blasted
yet the windshield stayed cold to the touch

above   the full moon
        large and bright in the sky
                so illuminated the icy fields
                        he could have driven without headlights

lunacy, really   what he says happened next
on the horizon   he saw

a sparkle of light   break   in the distance
        from a timid crack in the earth   an aperture
                something heavy opened   a beacon
                        spread   in the night   then a nose emerged

soundless   first, a tip   then a slim column lifted up   revealed itself

foot by foot   a minuteman
pulling clean from its shell
a needle unthreading itself

sparks followed   soundless   lifting in a spitting arc above
then growing small   out of sight   lost among the stars

he said   he barely kept the car on the road
he said   his hands spun the radio dial
        through talk & jazz
        all the late-night-preaching about   salvation
        fire & brimstone   end-of-days   revelation

he says   he scanned pop   rock   country
white noise   up and down the dial
he searched   for the breaking news
waiting to hear about the impact   what part of the world had fallen silent
but only the chatter continued   all night
he criss-crossed the roads and circled the dial

he knew   he didn't know   he said   he couldn't say

what he had seen   that winter night
in the high cold north   middle of nowhere
he drove the backroads until dawn, he said
waiting for the world to end.

III.   Frack

first the bakken   then the three forks formation   even deeper
    the oil patch, they call it
        two miles below the surface

oil embedded in shale
late devonian   remnants of the anoxic sea   the coastal carbonite layer
deposited when the middlewest was inner ocean

eighteen billion barrels, estimated rest there perhaps more light and tight
the largest oil find in north american history
    conflict-free oil, they say
    ending the dominance of energy-rich rogue nations

the boom began in montana, alberta
    then spread to north dakota
        drawn within our borders
            by a friendly change to the state tax code

now four thousand wells pump
    a million barrels a day, by some estimates
        thirty thousand new workers converging on small towns
        people housed in man camps
        some good people, some desperate, some dangerous

the talk is about the rise in crime—robberies, stabbings, domestic disputes
    a sidney, montana woman, early morning jogger, mother and math teacher
    grabbed from the side of the road
    later found strangled

(the murderers bought a shovel at walmart to bury her
    then returned it for a refund later
        that's how the police caught them).

so, the talk centers on the observable
    the damage to infrastructure
    the eyesore roads where there were no roads before
    the old highways, pitted and full of potholes   undriveable   dangerous

the speed of the oil and water trucks on the public roads
the rise in highway fatalities

to frack you must drill down
        through stratum, topsoil, sedimentary rock
            down through freshwater aquifers,
                to reach the dolomite   the source rock

drill vertically then horizontally to reach the shale
        injecting millions of gallons of water per frack
            laced with hundreds of chemicals (many linked to cancer)
                most of them proprietary to corporations
                    unknowable to ordinary citizens

unaskable, since the halliburton loophole (of 2005)
        exempted fracking from protections guaranteed to all citizens
            in the safe water drinking act (of 1974)

we knew   we couldn't say   we didn't know

except what's certain—benzene, toluene, ethylbenzene and xylene
        volatile organic compounds
            and diesel fuel (less than 1% per gallon) used on the bakken shale

plus, the radium inert in the rocks
brought back up in the fracking water
after it's made the long journey below to gather the oil
and brought topside to be separated out

then shipped to a wastewater center where it's *treated   cleaned*
        in condensate tanks, some of them lined, some unlined
            seeping into the ground, toxins evaporating into the air

what's left over, uncleanable
        trucked in water tankers to be disposed of   *reinjected*
            into the land previously known as *away.*

IV.   Quake

beyond the groundwater contamination
    now earthquakes in colorado, arkansas
        the swath of states between alabama and montana

a sixfold increase over twentieth century levels
        at least a dozen quakes last year in northern ohio
        one measuring up to 4.8 on the richter scale

speculation about the 30,000 disposal sites
    where fracking wastewater is deposited
        reinjected for final disposal
            into a deeper, unstable layer known as basement rock

and speculation about fracking itself
    the deep underground explosions to extract oil
        the water causing shifting plates, lubricating faults

        look for damage to homes
        look for reports of contaminated drinking water
        look for increases in breast cancer, miscarriages, birth defects

we knew   we couldn't say   we didn't know   ground zero

and this just in: the air force reports
        150 minutemen silos still rest underground
        honeycombed deep below
        ICBMs in northwestern north dakota
        embedded in the fracking zone

in news reports, the commander of the air base says,
    we certainly can co-exist with the oil industry
in news reports, the petroleum council vice president says,
    we're communicating about how we share our territory
in news reports, the air force commander says,
    the drilling frenzy has presented no ill-effects to the ICBMs

the public can be assured, they tell us
ultra-sensitive instruments possessed by the air force
can detect seismic activity as far away as mexico
capable of tracking even the slight vibrations
caused by the simplest of thunderstorms

V.   Lament

north dakota   i'm worried about you
the companies you keep   all these new friends   north dakota
    beyond the boom, beyond the precious resources
        do you really think they care what becomes of you

north dakota   you used to be the shy one
enchanted secret land loved by only a few   north dakota

when i traveled away and told people i belonged to you   north dakota
    your name rolled awkwardly from their tongues
        a mouth full of rocks, the name of a foreign country

north dakota   you were the blushing wallflower
the natural beauty, nearly invisible, always on the periphery
north dakota   *the least visited state in the union*

now everyone knows your name   north dakota
the blogs and all the papers are talking about you   even *60 minutes*
i'm collecting your clippings   north dakota
the pictures of you from space
    the flares of natural gas in your northern corner
        like an exploding supernova
            a massive city where no city exists
                a giant red blight upon the land

and those puncture wounds   north dakota   take care of yourself
the injection sites   I've see them on the maps
four thousand active wells   one every two miles

all your indicators are up   north dakota
    eighteen billion barrels, some estimates say

more oil than we have water to extract
    more oil than we have atmosphere to burn

north dakota you could run the table right now you could write your ticket
    so, how can i tell you this?   north dakota, your politicians

are co-opted (or cowards or bought-out or honest and thwarted)
they're lowering the tax rate for oil companies
they're greasing the wheels that need no greasing
they're practically giving the water away
they have opened you up and said, *come in   take everything*

north dakota   dear sleeping beauty   please, wake up

what will become of your sacred places,
what will become of the prairie dog,
the wolf, the wild horses, the eagle,
the meadowlark, the fox, the elk,
the pronghorn, the rare mountain lion,
the roads, the air, the topsoil,
your people, your people,
what will become of the water?

north dakota   who will ever be able to live with you
once this is all over   i'm speaking to you now
as one wildcat girl   to another   be careful   north dakota

Wild Thyme

Buoy

And so you came to realize that a married man
is like a drowning victim, when you find him

drenched, adrift and unhappy in the vast ocean
of his marriage. And won't you always be the one

to spot him—a floating speck on the horizon,
flapping his arms for rescue, desperate mouth

ringing an O above the rolling crests and waves.
You on the high dry deck of the cruise ship

in your crisp white shorts and espadrilles.
Aren't you the beacon, aren't you the life preserver.

And when you jump into the sea salt foam,
if only for a refreshing swim, don't you understand

that he will seize upon you, strong buoyant
swimmer that you are, grab your shoulders,

pull your head under with his weight, so dense
in the water. And down among the reefs

and coral, with your new copper-coin eyes,
you will see then how he rides upon the shoulders

of his water-breathing sea horse wife,
and his mermaid mistresses, those water nymph

former lovers, and a whole tag-team pyramid
of three-breasted women who tried

over the years to save him. Even then,
next time, when you see another one

go under, does it give you pause,
does it stop you from jumping in—

no, not once, not ever.

Wild Thyme

I took the photographs, naturally, as the other poets
fell backwards into wild thyme, too worried
about appearing the tourist or ruining my clothes

in the phryngana, the zone between mountain
and sea, wood and water. On the rented boat
to Antiparos, as the others slipped into wet suits,

pulled on squeaky flippers, rolled into azure depths
with Panayotis, the marine biologist, I stayed
on the moored boat with whiskery Captain Giorgos

nursing my salty old grudges against water.
On the south shore of the island, when invited
to sing into the mouth of the sea caves that echo

the ancient world back, I had only this pop tune
to offer (I can't bear to name it). Between Lefkes
and Marpissa, where the Byzantine trail empties

down to the sea, when the old man with hair
like a wild bird's nest and a toothless collapsing
chin saw me, an American, enter the chapel

he guarded, he shouted, *Ah, George Bush!*
and my only response was, *I didn't do it!*
(meaning, vote for him) which made all

the other Americans laugh. At Marathi,
where the mountain opens to marble quarries
so translucent that the Venus de Milo,

the temples on Delos, and Napoleon's tomb
are carved from it, as the guide distributed
the headlamps for our underground excursion,

he had to ask, *Now, is anyone here claustrophobic?*
And I had to answer, *Well, yes*, because
I would never depend upon tourists

to pull my limp and breathless body
from any dark crevasse. So I guarded
the entrance as the others descended,

sat back to study the guidebooks.
Did you know that 150,000 slaves mined
these quarries. They say a bas relief

above one opening depicts Pan cavorting
with Nymphs. Did you know the thyme
that grows on this mountainside feeds

bees that make rare, wild honey, the color
of amber. Aromatic and savory, they say,
with the taste of white pepper, dates, and fruit,

although I have never dared to taste it.

The Oud

It traveled to me from Damascus
    shipped in a plywood box
resembling a baby's coffin.
    Inside the rough latches,
the tiny instrument's long thin neck,
    its bent-back pegbox,
and staved gourd of a stomach
    looked like the resting body
of a goose, exhausted
    from the forced migration
across the Atlantic and Mediterranean.

Forebear of the lute and guitar,
    what hands must have played you
before my graceless fumblings,
    what ancient music sounded
through your strings. And how strange
    the moist new air must have seemed.

In truth, the oud did not last six months.
    First, the neck failed to hold
the instrument in tune. One-by-one
    the ribs sprang loose
from the pear-shaped soundbox.
    Soon, the spruce top
pulled free from the cavernous body
    as if something inside
the instrument insisted on its freedom.

But that first morning
    something happened, so odd
I now recall—
    when I burned sage,
passed a smudge over
    the instrument
to clear its path to this new world,
    as I turned to leave the room,

a note sounded from its strings,
    an audible note rang out
I swear. One note, loud and clear
    with no hand or fingers touching
the neck or strings, without a pick
    or a plectrum in sight.

Whisker Meditations

1.

When I told my fiancé's mother about my persistent, recurring whisker—lower right, underside of my chin—she smiled sideways, said, "Be glad it's only one."

2.

I was parked in the lot outside Bed, Bath & Beyond with my then-husband. I was applying lipstick in the mirror the first time I spotted it—my whisker enjoying a stretch of unchecked growth.

It was hot in the car. We were laughing. My husband tried to pull it out with his fingertips. When that failed, he offered to tweeze it with his teeth. What an act of extreme devotion. It makes me wonder why I ever let him go.

3.

It begins, a smooth bump on the skin that you must worry for days with your fingertips. Then, a small nub, slight friction in the follicle, nothing visible. Hours pass, days. You forget. Then one day you catch it in silhouette or sunlight—a long tendril like a pliable scrap of piano wire sprung from your chin.

4.

My friend Jenny tells me about one night after she and Colin made love. Lying there, sweaty, happy, Colin spotted a long brown hair on Jenny's chest—his hair, he thought. When he tried to pick it off, the skin lifted, the follicle resisted. It was connected. "Get it off me," Jenny screamed. "Get it off!"

5.

This sliver of iron ore spun from the lava core of the earth, one thin chin wire rising through Cambrian, Devonian, up through continental shelves, bedrock, shale, topsoil. This tendril—manganese, copper, platinum—must have pierced my heel, threaded my first step, wound around tendons, up shin, thigh, groin, traveled through heart, breast, throat to arrive here on my chin in my fortieth year.

6.

Sometimes in meetings at work, I catch myself stroking my sad whisker when contemplating problems. I better understand now the gestures of my bearded colleagues who, over the years, have cradled their chins, stroked with the grain, against the grain, or, when really perplexed, vigorously scratched a stubbled cheek.

7.

In the bathroom of a four-star hotel—marble shower, terrazzo floors—I turn on the lighted magnifying mirror hanging near the vanity. Never mind crow's feet, enlarged pores, the natural exigencies of age.

But, oh, in the magnifying glass, under that terrifying light—constellations of age spots, catastrophe of eyebrows, oh, whisker. All the while my fiancé is knocking on the frosted glass door. *What are you doing in there?*

8.

And now my whisker has attracted an evil twin, albino white, emerging from the doorway of the neighboring pore. How long, how long, will it be before the rest of the family arrives— the older brother, the in-laws and parents, not to mention the car full of California cousins.

9.

To pluck it, you must stand by the window, blinds open in full light with a tweezers and a hand mirror. Try to tuck yourself behind the billow of the curtain. No need for you to star in a YouTube video entitled, "My Crazy Old Neighbor Lady Plucks Her Whisker Again."

10.

You'll never get it on the first try or the second. You have to poke around. Then one day, the tweezer's edge will land, small suction as the follicle releases. When it happens to me, I hold the whisker up in the light, say, *Got it! You bastard!*

A small moment of satisfaction followed by silence, vacuous air, contemplating the many hours and days, the many weeks it will take for this grave act to be undone.

lake effect

snow for days   let it
    the weather woman
        is always wrong   we rise

these pearl white mornings
    made warm by your long back
        east of lake michigan

unexpected   always coming
    great crystal flakes
        float outside your windows

white pine branches lowered
    heavy with snow   we rise
        to the meteorologist's apologies

this upland peninsula
    so shaped like a paw
        or an oven mitt

people will raise their hands
    a kind of swearing to
        and point to the spot

where they're from   this place
    in the heart of the palm
        where I found you

a bit left of center
    lake effect   people around here say
        to things that happen

all the things   wonderful or strange
    they can never hope to
        predict or explain.

Another Day on Earth

Good morning, I shout to the jogger
who passes me on the boardwalk
because it's sunny and lakes country.

Yes, he says. *It's a good day to be above ground!*
He speaks out of the side of his mouth
like a tough guy or a stroke victim

or a tough guy who's survived a stroke
which brings my father to mind. I look down
to avoid the cracks between the slats.

Beside me, Lake Superior waves its heavy
blue arms. I watch the disappearing backside
of the jogger. His headband matches

his wristbands—white terrycloth and tight.
His limp is quick, but not fast enough
for the ferocious pumping of arms.

His too tiny running shorts and tank top
reveal too much bruised and mottled skin
like parchment bearing signs of recent illness.

After my father died, the nerve of everything
that moved and breathed offended me
as he slept deep in a cold blue suit.

At the cemetery, as the casket lowered,
we all stared down in silence, except for
the whine of hydraulics. And the second

gears ceased their crawling—that very moment—
mourners turned and started talking
of weather and crops. I'm told my father

used to joke at funerals, *why does someone
always have to die for us to get together?*
He was good at that. Better than me.

Laughing into the teeth of death.

mother, in pictures

mother, at two   propped on the running board
    of the brand-new model t truck   swaddled
        in a black wool coat and fur hat   mother

posing by the peonies wearing a white crochet tam
    mother, outside   holding a ukulele   a baton   a baby doll

mother posing with tricycle   later, with bicycle
    mother in a black french beret
        mother posing in her good cotton school dress
           behind her, the long unbroken horizon

    years later great aunt martha would say,
    your ma sure thought she got something when she had you

mother, at five   holding leroy, her baby brother   the one good day
    the blustery sky   his crying red eyes
        born in may, he died in november

mother with a wagon, hauling her dolls
    feeding the lambs with a nipple bottle
        posing with two white dogs   with a black horse

then a third child, another boy   mother was eleven
    the midwife told grandpa to go for a doctor
        twenty-five miles to napoleon, no doctor available
        thirty miles to steele, no doctor available

mother said she hid in the barn, covered her ears to muffle grandma's screams
    the boy was named donald
        born with a broken arm and collarbone
           he lasted two days

your ma sure thought she got something when she had you.

mother, in a white dress holding her lutheran catechism
    mother, in winter, twenty years old in a tight white sweater
        hugging her knees on the front steps
           a windmill in the background   mother
              she hasn't met any of us yet

Poor You

Back when we were still together, it seemed
my ex-boyfriend could never lose anything.
Car keys, dollar bills, everything that fell from

his charmed pockets floated back. *Lucky us.*
Check books dropped in grocery store parking lots
delivered to our front door by Good Samaritans

before the ice cream melted. Perhaps this is why
he treated me with such benign neglect, forgetting
how the slippery dime of me could work through

the stitches of silk pockets. Once, at the therapist's
he handed the Kleenex box to me with this look
on his face, like *poor you*, like I was a catastrophe

under glass. *Oh, poor us.* It reminded me of a cartoon
I'd seen in the paper of two men in a sinking canoe.
The guy in the front end is submerged, taking in water,

already drowning. The guy in the back of the canoe
is tipped up high and dry. In the caption, he's thinking,
Boy, am I glad I wasn't on that end of the boat.

Interest

To hold love in one's hands like capital
like a fluid animal, best in motion,

then pass it along with a bit skimmed off,
that's the theory of love and interest.

Last night in the dream my first husband
said, *I dream of you.* Odd in a dream to hear

what another dreams, odder still to receive
the offer so many years after the desire.

This is how love most resembles money,
everyone willing to give you the thing

most wished for, once it's no longer needed.
Like those sprinklers we ran through

during the downpour in the Bitterroots—
no one could tell us how to turn them off.

All night, in bed we heard them *fust, fust*
against dripping willows. The next morning,

the besotted lawn, the driver waiting
to take you to the airport. Your hand

on your heart, for lack of words,
as we kissed before our final parting.

To the Woman Who Tore the Word "Husband" from the *Oxford English Dictionary*

Surely it was a wife who removed
the pages beginning with *hurtle*
and ending with *hush*, while the word,

husband, lurked somewhere in between,
ripped, judging from the jagged edges
and stuffed in a coat pocket

to be smuggled to a kitchen table,
to a fierce fight under glaring light,
to be read aloud and pointed at

and served up as solid evidence.
The missing pages now replaced
in grainy photocopy by some librarian,

so that other confused or angry
women can continue to check for
true meanings of the word. *Husband*,

finding its roots in "house" and
"bound," as in, a man who owns
his house and land, or the master

of the household (now obsolete),
or a tiller of the ground (also obsolete),
or a male animal kept for breeding

(rare, OED insists). In the history
of the language, he's had many names
and occupations—tiller of soil, cultivator,

the steward who manages his affairs
with skill and thrift. He's out there,
the husband, each day redefining

the word that follows *hurtless, hurtsome.*

Memorabilia

—Roger Maris Museum, West Acres Shopping Mall, Fargo, North Dakota

Across from Nails Pro and Forever 21
behind a corner of glass, Roger Maris
swings without ceasing and rounds bases
on an endless tape loop of home runs—
57, 58, 59, 60—leading to run number 61
in the year 1961, the homer that broke
Babe Ruth's 1927 record. His trophies,
autographed baseballs, and signed bats
rest under a portrait of his golden beauty
near the display of authentic jerseys,
his Sultan of Swat crowns, and replicas
of a Yankees locker and stadium seat.
Maris died of lymphatic cancer at age 51
in a Houston hospital. "I still see him
in my dreams," Mickey Mantle said.
The Baseball Hall of Fame holds the ball
he hit off Tracy Stallard in the '61 Series,
his No. 61 bat, and his No. 9 Yankees
jersey, but his body was brought home
to Fargo to be buried on the north side
at the Holy Cross Cemetery on 32nd Avenue.
His tombstone, a square of black granite
mounted to resemble a baseball diamond.

Bookmobile

To be saved by books, to be allowed to file
in twos away from Sister Paula's math class,

to climb those three small steps off the curb,
and be met by the smell of glue, old paper,

leather bindings. To lay my hands on
thin volumes with titles other than *The Lives*

of the Saints—a miracle. And that woman
a saint, who steered the big wheel and roared

the loaded van to our school each Friday.
I do not recall the plots or the people

in those books, though I read them all—
every word in every book in each tall stack

that I hauled in small arms down the steps,
making the final blind hop to the curb,

then back to the rigors of six times eight
equals. After school, I'd crawl into bed

with those books, the weight of them
spread all around me. Mother washed

the bedding each Friday, and the combination
was unbearable—heaven—pages turned

by unknown hands and the fresh air
smell of clean sheets. The rows of black words

on heavy paper, concrete proof of things
calling me from beyond the parochial.

Purse

They say pickpockets brush past victims first
to observe the unconscious protective gesture—
where the hand goes after soft contact reveals

the precise location of the wallet or passport.
Some memories from childhood, I'm realizing,
are no longer felt or known, but live only in poems,

stored there when my memory held like a purse
whose drawstrings I pulled open and closed.
My mother's dreams of my late father

are often pecuniary. In the car en route
to somewhere, she'll realize she's forgotten
her purse. *Don't worry*, he will say, *I have money*.

Who knows where loves hides in the enclosures
of marriage. The first time my fiance's son
sneezed and reached out to me for a tissue,

I understood why mothers carry such big purses.
Because memory is a sieve, separating the coarse
from the fine. Because memory is a seine, catching

and releasing. Like my grandfather's brook trout—
do I remember it from the actual rainbow display
as he posed that day beside the bright curtains

or from the snapshot in Grandmother's album?
And the reedy timbre of my father's voice,
can I retrieve it now as an acoustic artifact,

as a thing my ear can still hear, or only
in the playback recording of my own voice,
the copy he made in me. *Oh goodness,*

my cousin will say when I go home to visit,
you sure have your father's mannerisms. It's a thing
that people will observe, but you could never

see yourself. Then today, something strange—
playing with the puppies, I felt my lips purse,
a gesture to contain happiness too soft and pure

for release into laughter. And I recognized it
as the look I saw on my father's face watching me
growing up. Only I'm wearing it now on my own body,

this muted expression of my father's love.

News Flash

"This is a substantial find as diamonds of this size
are a very rare occurrence," Nare's CEO Charles Mostert said.
  —*Mail & Guardian*, April 22, 2006

One cape yellow diamond, octahedron-shaped, 235 carats,
was found in the Schmidstdrift mine, an alluvial riverbed

outwash near Kimbereley, South Africa, by a three-week-old
start up company named Nare Diamonds Limited who re-opened

the mine—closed for three years by the previous company,
(unnamed, in all accounts) who labored there for years,

who went bankrupt mining gems of 1.14 carats or less.
The report says, twenty-one days after resuming work

in the Schmidstdrift, Nare Diamonds found the 235 carat
diamond, cape yellow, octahedron, the size of a hen's egg,

rough-cut and shining amidst the mine's erosion deposits.
This small morning news flash, scrolling across my screen,

returns me to my desk, to the bottom left drawer,
to the gray green notebook, and what lies buried there.

Back When We All Got Along

Everyone's thinner, less worn in the face.
The children are all on the wrong laps,
disorderly pyramid of family spreading

up the front steps. The sun is bright,
the lawn so green. Father grasps
the wrought iron rail on the top landing,

his usual amused smirk, his waistband
pulled high under armpits. Mother looks
so young, a sister among daughters.

The smallest grandson squirms on her lap.
Wish I could insert myself beside them.
I was missing all those years, on the road

playing music. My brother-in-law, Al
is missing too, probably visiting family
in Oakes. And my second-oldest sister

has said something funny from behind
the camera to get the kids to make faces—
stuck-out tongues, googly-eyed monsters.

Grandma stands on the lawn beside them—
her delighted smile, her hands folded over
her stomach. Gotthelf is with her,

the man she married after Grandpa died,
who is already senile or soon will be.
Soon, too, three children for my brother

and his young wife. Plus, the discovery
that the other brother-in-law, the one
posed high on the landing with Father,

is using more than his fine carpentry skills
to renovate the kitchen, bathroom, deck,
and sunroom of the woman in town

with the traveling husband. But not today,
today looks perfect, except for the wrinkle
of the youngest daughter's absence.

I want to bless them from this distance.
Debbie is like the wind, they often say of me,
You never know when she will blow into town.

China: 5,000 Years

Guggenheim Museum Exhibition, 1998

not the jade ornament of a pig-dragon   or the lamp
        in the shape of a goose holding a fish
not the bronze buckle ornament of a dancer with cymbals
        or the nephrite jade carving of a winged horse
                all from the second century B.C.E.

not the chime with a crouching dragon carving
        from 1600 B.C.E. or the gilt bronze
rearing dragon from the eighth century

not the Neolithic goblet with eggshell walls so delicate
        or the eleven-headed bust of Avalokitesvara,
looking eleven times compassionate, or the Buddhist
        ritual objects—a carved turtle, a pillbox

not the Ming dynasty silk paintings with mountains
        that look like dragons
or the earthenware squatting musician with dimples
        and a drum from 25 B.C. who looks
as modern as the busker you saw on the street today

not the dragon-shaped jade pendants from
        the fourth century B.C.E.
that make you wonder about the marvelous lapels or blouses
        of the ancient people who could have worn such things

which gets you thinking about the cave of your own people
        where they must have been squatting at that time
                drinking out of streams, gnawing meat off bones
with no clock or mirror or comb or pen
        or compass or gilded silver tea utensils
                certainly, not even tea or calligraphy

none of this hits you until the Indian restaurant
        on Columbus Avenue
where you sit by a big window and watch the stream
        of faces push by and perhaps you've had

too much wine, and garlic naan, and mughlai chicken,
        and maybe the ragas aren't helping either,
the sitars and tablas circling around a five-note melody

and that's when something starts to well up in you
        —you hope you can make it back to the hotel—
so you ask the waiter for your bill, but instead
        he brings you dessert, a small custard
in an oval bowl which he offers in cupped hands
        for your inspection
                saying, for you, on the house

and you try to say thank you, to register your delight
        but instead, something starts to come out,
a deluge, real crying, real shoulder-rocking sobs
        the napkin clutched to your face
                mascara smeared on white linen

all of which alarms the waiter, who has bent down
        to you now, and the two women dining
                in the table next to you
have rushed to your side asking, is it something we said?

        No, no, between sobs, you try to tell them
about the exhibit of 5,000 years of Chinese history
        about the smooth five-petaled porcelain bowl
from the 10th century and the funerary objects carved
        in the shapes of laughing dogs

but all you can get out, really, is the thing about
        the terra cotta warriors, the soldier,
the military officers, the general, and their horse and cart
        to represent the other 6,000 figures discovered
in Pit 1 in the Shaanxi province, the way they looked
        so lost in the Guggenheim without their spears,
swords, or crossbows, with their hands frozen
        after centuries as if still holding weapons

but mostly, it was their faces—
    how you realized real people must have
posed for each statue, real people from 200 B.C.E.
    each with unique noses, hair plaits,
shapes of eyes, curves of cheekbone—

and how they were all so dead now,
    how they'd all been dead
        for such an incredibly long time.

From Sweetness | 2002

In memory of C.W. Truesdale,
editor and friend

The open palm of desire wants everything,
wants everything, wants everything.
      —Paul Simon, "Further to Fly"

In a Cool Dark Tongue

Other Knowledge

Somewhere in this hot city he sleeps,
tangled in rough sheets, his body

twisted in the shape of a question.
If he knocked on this loosely hung door

I would remove the chain and answer
all he asks, my skin scrubbed clean,

smelling of green apples and lemons.
How I want to trace with my hands

the slow curve of his back. Lover,
I would say, lie down on the cool

sheets and let me wash the salt from
your skin. How long have we held

our breath swimming deep strokes
to meet in these murky waters, how long

have we heard this music, soft and dark
as the inside of a womb. You say

you're from a large southern city,
but I have other knowledge.

I rattled you out of the sand
with my shaker noisemakers,

one egg in each hand, dancing
in circles, chanting the names

we use only in sleep. Did you know
the Aboriginal man dreams the spirit

of a child then comes home to love
his wife, saying, Today I saw a child,

and now I have planted it in your womb.
If you knock, the chains will dissolve

in your hands. Inside, find me brewing
this mixture of spearmint and cloves.

Lie back, let me trace this bayleaf, soft
as a feather down the smooth line

of your stomach. In a cool dark tongue,
perhaps it will find words for us to speak,

saying, Love this woman, you've been
adrift in the open sea for too long.

How Bad News Comes

A telephone rings
like an emergency
in a room down
the hall. I think
of the one to whom
bad news is coming.
At the market,
she touches fruit.
Driving home,
she strums her fingers
on the steering wheel.
Humming with the radio
she thinks of her lover,
the one she's left
behind, or the one
she will see again,
remembers the soft heat
of his breath, the urgency
of his belly against hers.
This is the way life
insists on itself, his scent
still on her as she reaches
for the phone. Happy
to catch it in mid-ring,
she comes through
the door, leaves her keys
dangling in the lock.
She leans in, unclips
an earring, to hear
the voice on the other end
saying, *I've got some
bad news*, feeling
in that long moment
before the words come,

the difference between
the way it was
and the way
it will be, that moment
before the groceries
fall to the floor.

On Lake Superior

What returns us to these shores, the promise
of fish, something silver flashing through our veins.

I walk the long pier, past the rollerbladers,
bowlegged in their knee pads, past the children

tossing popcorn to gulls. On the edge
of this great inner ocean, we are all tourists,

a light circling overhead, calling us like sailors,
home. And we are lovers, kissing against the rail,

turning our faces to our collars in the cold
spray of waves. A fisherman looks at water

and sees something waiting to be caught.
My father, who is nowhere now, would turn

and declare Superior and all her rocky shores
an absolute waste. A farmer sees the world

that way, as so much land in need of planting.
I've abandoned despair, that miserable lifeboat.

The water does not care enough to care
nothing for me. From the street, the creak

of a carriage, horses' hooves on cobblestone,
that old, old poetry. The wind blows tones

tonight, a saxophone, on the boardwalk,
breathing in, breathing out, the blue smoke

of a song I know but can't recall. A stone
rides deep in my belly. Soon I must return

to my small river, go down to the shore
and beat my clothes against the hardness,

open my throat and try to make a song
from the long ago row of notes.

Beating up the Brother

Because he was a single stalk
of sweet corn in a prairie of sisters,
because we were seven, nine,

eleven, and twelve, and he
was only ten—the middle one,
the fulcrum our farm rested on.

Because he was too cute
and wore short pants, little hand
in the cookie jar, little shrug

and grin. Because his buzz cut
felt like a freshly mowed lawn
when we drove our hands over it,

because Mom and Dad left us alone
some nights to watch Ed Sullivan
or the Miss America Pageant,

because no beauty from Dakota
ever won, or advanced
to the final round of ten.

Because we were a gaggle
of girls, expected to fly away
and he would stay to plow

the land after we were gone.
Because he was the only boy,
sweet-natured and forgiving

as Jesus under our fists. Because
he was the brother, had that part
we thought of as extra, that part

we had never seen but knew existed.

My Husband, a City Boy, Decides to Buy a Truck

When I find him, he's lying on the bed
with magazines, surrounded by glossy
spreads, the fleshy airbrushed tones

of break-your-neck beautiful pick up
trucks, their commercials promising
added legroom, adventure in ownership,

and deliverance from all life's hard, stuck
places. Rock guitars chime with whiskey
voices about narrow misses, rugged

times survived, all thanks to the solid
dependability of a 4 x 4. This is how
it will be: you arrive in your truck

(AKA, the rock) loaded down with fun-
loving girls wearing tank tops and short,
fringed cut-offs. They hop from the cab

tossing their glossy hair to find the next
available good time. In the back are guitars
and amplifiers, and silver kegs full of

piss-warm beer. Believe me, you'll kiss
yourself then for having the horsepower.
This is the new truck, he says. Gone

are the days of gun racks and roped deer,
tires kicking up tufts of dirt, the dark
shrinking silhouette of a cowboy hat

as the truck climbs the last rise. For me,
it was hay bales, straw bales, alfalfa bales,
rocks, rocks and more rocks, cranky

stick-shifts, slippery clutches, feet barely
reaching the pedals, driving lunch out
to Dad in the august fields, dust and sweat-

slicked seats, the smell of oil and tractor
grease, the thunk and tumble of gas cans
rolling in the back. Listen, I tell him.

Here are three things I'd like to never
again do—wear a seed cap, live in
a trailer park, and own a pickup truck.

Eventually I add, *wear safety orange,*
to the list, but that's years later
and another story altogether.

The Watkins Man

Ever since the Kirby man sold Grandmother
the Dual Sanitronic by shampooing
to sparkling brilliance a five-inch circle

in the dead walking center of her carpet,
so that she had to buy the magnificent beast
with all its twenty-five purring parts

(the linoleum sweeper, the edge cleaner,
and the motorized attachment that doubles
as a belt sander) to get the rest of the rug

to match, we are not at home to salesmen.
A good thing about living in the country,
Mother says, is you can see trouble coming

from miles away. When the funnel of dust
rises along the section line, like the white-gloved
finger of God, we know it's the Watkins man

in his spackled green van full of boar's hair
brushes and clouded ammonia solutions
that bristle and slosh to the road's dips

and curves. Get down, mother yells.
We suck it up and dive like infantry
at Guadalcanal, our noses pressed

into mother's waxy hardwood. Outside,
the Watkins man, his nose pickled,
his pores deep as canyons, knocks

his hamhock fists on our weatherbeaten,
never-locked door. We wait, twelve eyes
breathless, staring, for the screen door's

report against the frame, for the slippy slap
of shoes receding. Wait for the car door
slam's ricochet off the barn, the worried

zing of his engine, the neck-craning
turnaround crunch of gravel, before we rise,
dust ourselves, collapse together in laughter

and relief. We know he's just an honest man
trying to make a living, but he shouldn't
have tried to show Mother, that one time,

the fishy handfuls of dust, the sloughed-off
human scales that lurk infectious in our
mattresses. He just shouldn't have done that.

Envy of Origins

Wipe the dust from your face
gravel road girl, your childhood spent,
not on Wordsworth or Keats,

but on the intricate hoisting
of hay bales to a hip.
How you were made

for lifting—books pulled
from your hands, shoulders
pushed outdoors to fresh air.

you walked the gravel roads,
endless miles, eyes cast down,
reading the stones' etched

faces. Lift your eyes now,
move aside for the poetess
who storms through in long skirts

boasting of days whiled away
with Auden, evenings spent
with Edna St. Vincent Millay,

all the rainy mornings,
and dusty libraries of childhood.
Admire the antique earrings

plucked from a safe back east
(where all the family heirlooms
are kept). With not a piece

of china or a silver engraving
to recommend you, what are your
treasures—the grandmother

who left the world screaming
bloody childbirth, the grandfather
crossing the Volga under cover

of darkness, their bones buried
deep in the vault of earth. How
will you raise them? Think

how you invented games
as a child, playing catch
with yourself, when no one

was there to throw the ball
back, recall the loud whack
against the side of the barn,

the hard thunk of return
in your palm. And no matter
how you complicated things,

spinning tricky english,
throwing odd angles, always
the ball found its point

of origin, always your hips
divined the trajectory,
always your hands knew

where they must be next.

The Falling Man

How I wanted to touch the stitching
of his wrist brace that summer he fell
from his bike. Perched on the stoop
with his backpack, he showed me

the crisscross and I wanted to undo it,
lay my hands on the perfect hairline
fracture. And how I wanted to trace
the faint stitching scar on his shin,

cauterize it with my own heat the next
summer when he also fell from his bike,
the rusty chain breaking free, the toothy
links circling his ankle. And though

I wondered about him always falling
from bikes, I admired him for being man
enough to cry in front of the women,
and for later telling me, a woman

he didn't know wouldn't laugh,
that he had cried. And so I took to
reading his horoscope every morning
wondering what kind of a day

he was having, and I grew jealous
of the shower water rolling in clear
innocuous rivulets down his body,
and I hated the impervious cotton sheets

that touched him each morning as he rolled over,
that first moment of waking, reaching for himself,
as any man does. And I envied the warm
lucky life of his backpack, and the strings

of his work apron that tied, so thoughtlessly
around his waist, and the long, looping straps
of his tank top that conspired to expose
the ripples and flanks of his chest which

I studied for many long minutes that night
of his twenty-fourth birthday before thrusting
out my hand in stiff arm congratulations
to avert the hug that was certain to give me

heart failure. And when I pointed to
the slim scar high on his forehead, he said
he had fallen from a great height as a child
and I said, *oh, now I'm starting to see all*

your faults, which made both of us laugh
out loud. This man, so steady on his feet
around me, those years I waited for him
to waver, to trip, to swagger, to sway.

Those years I waited for him to fall
headlong into my strange wild arms.

My Catholic Tongue

She's like a surly bank robber this new hygienist,
in her face mask and goggles, nervous about
silent alarms and the time this is all taking.

She cracks my mouth like a vault, scans
the perimeter as if for surveillance equipment.
As soon as she's in, she taps the gleaming

gold fillings and runs the scaler across my gums,
her deep pricks looking for redness, soreness,
the telltale signs of the dreaded gingivitis,

so she can call the dentist, drilling and tapping
in the other room, and, in an important voice
say, *Here, take a look at what I found.* My tongue

follows her like an ineffectual security guard
in a crisp uniform and badge, with no gun
or holster. Armed with simple vigilance,

the curious tip is wrestled to the floor,
held by the long arm of her tiny probing mirror.
Hard at work now, the curette chips away.

Ripping plaque, pieces flying free like plaster
off a concealing wall, she asks, in a cool voice,
Do I floss each week. My catholic tongue,

ever the stoolie, wants to confess, but waggles
Un-hungh. I fade and lapse under the pressure
of her instruments, the sharp prong of the scaler

returning for clean up, scoping out the crevices,
the dark places where all treasure can be found,
the mirror's bright aluminum head craning side

to side, saying, *Are you a cavity, are you a cavity,
are you*, looking for my dirty den of neglect.
The sympathetic nodding hook of the curette

returning, saying, *See, we could have been friends.*
My tongue lying low, hissing silently to itself
the precise location of the motherlode.

Light Sweet Crude

At midnight in the produce section
I think about the old woman on CNN
who stood on the rubble of her
white stone house and raged
at the camera in an Arabic tongue,
the cords of her neck straining. *Civilian,*

she screamed, *civilian.* Her only English word.
Inside, children lay crushed in beds
like corsages in bibles. The camera scans
the wreckage—dishes and cups broken
into fragments, a water gourd once round
and smooth as a baby's head, now smashed

entirely open. Halfway across the world
they're dropping bombs. All night,
from inside the deep land cushion
of the middle west I watch this great
fireworks display of war. All day, at work
the talk is of how many sorties flown,

how many Xs obliterated, how many people
ran like ants out of the crosshairs
of a missile. As the ten-millionth
screw in the great roaring machinery
of business, my job is not to question
the dropping of bombs. Halfway across

the world, where light sweet crude
bubbles up from the sand, they are
dropping bombs, and tonight
in the produce section, I'm struck
by the violence of even this fruit—
the lengths my country will go

to deliver the juicy acres of peaches,
kiwi and grapes, the seven kinds
of apples in February, all laid out
in polished rows for my inspection.
Halfway across the world
they're dropping bombs

on my behalf. Get that fruit
away from me. I will not eat it.

Within Moments

Sarajevo, 1994

Some French photographer has captured
this moment—a woman in a gray coat,

fallen face down to the pavement,
moments after the mortar rounds

have stopped. From the triangle
of her scarf, a pool of blood spreads

gray and thick as oil. Her boots
are turned inward, her shoulders

crumpled under like some ruined
and forgotten thing. See how quickly

she has joined the legion of the dead.
Moments ago she was a woman

hurrying to an errand. Now
the boy with a gray bag in his hands

climbing the stairs does not stop
to check her pulse. Even as his eyes

glance back, his right leg veers out
of the photo. And the two men

in uniform coming up from the dark
subway, lift their legs and look at her

with the same mark of exhaustion.
Later, someone will remove her

to the morgue where attendants
will find a message still nestled

in her pocket, the reason she is out
today, to deliver this letter

to the Red Cross for a granddaughter
on the other side of the fighting.

Thank God, the note will read,
that you are all alive and well,

and thank God, that we
are all alive and well.

From Sweetness

What was the taste of him beneath
the sprinkles that fell from pastries,
the eclairs and bismarcks, the jelly

donuts in the box on the table
in the room behind the Line of Fire
shooting range (don't ask) where we talked

for hours. The sugary blue
half moons and thin yellow stars
that he dabbed with his wet finger

and brought to his mouth time and
(agonizing) time again, the sweetness
dissolving on his tongue as rounds

of ammo popped off. Outside the door,
men in goggles in a lock-legged stance
aimed at silhouettes, intruders

flying toward us on long pulleys,
tattered and riddled with bullet holes
to be examined for accuracy of firing.

And with me so terrified of hand guns
and small talk, what held me there
next to his velvet presence, content

to imagine the collection of sprinkles
dissolving on his tongue (all the while
thanking god for my excellent

peripheral vision). And where
was the word (yes) on my tongue
in the parking lot, when he asked

in his no-one-but-you voice
who wanted to go for burgers,
causing me to recall someone

who waited, hungry, at home.
Amazing, how the body recovers,
finds the car keys in the messy bag,

the jagged teeth of the ignition,
grinds for reverse, first, navigates
the long left loop onto the freeway.

When will we know if we've made
a mistake? Impossible to count
the times I've turned back, slipped

my body into the booth, felt
the length of his thigh lining mine,
imagined the thin fries delivered,

crisp and sizzling in their checkered
basket for devouring, watched
their small journey, one by one,

from the dab of ketchup to the tip
of his tongue. Sometimes my own hand
reaches in to touch his wrist, directs

the oily gold from his fingertips
to my lips. So bad for me (I know)
so good. The taste of salt

that follows so much sweetness.

Our Gold and Yellow Making

Drats

What becomes of them, the cousins
who call late at night, a little drunk
they admit, and wanting to talk about

the crimes of the first lady, their hopes
for her future imprisonment. We are bound
together by this blood, the love our fathers

never spoke. What do teenagers care of curses
before birth, that old-land-brother-hunger?
The earth was dirt to us, and the ripened

wheat singing to mudflaps on his father's pickup,
on my father's land was background noise
to backroads drives, where we parked to talk

of gradations of blood relation to the radio's
lighted dial. Is it too late to recall that word
we discovered scratched on the chemistry

desk's obsidian surface—*drats*—carved,
we theorized, by some dome-headed farmboy
destined to firebomb into the south Pacific

or be sucked through the combine's irresistible
conveyor. And when Mr. Dewald's questions
about the shared properties of matter eluded us,

we would mouth that word, *drats*, a bunsen
burner flaring between us, and understand
everything about fusion. Revolutions undo us,

our blood divided and divided again. No wonder
we held tight the twining taper. Here is the empty
motel room he calls from, twenty years later,

the pop top hissing in silence, here is the spout
of alcohol and politics. Here we are, cousin,
out in the world, just as you predicted,

among strangers who would never guess
our secrets. What remains for me to confess—
the children I left you to never have?

Our fathers lie together now in the rise
near the field where we lay. See how things
come around? When you call, if you like,

we can work the dark nubby root between us,
gorge ourselves at the table of family hurt.
But don't slur and ask me that question again:

Hey, is this where all the cool people live?

My Father's Wallet

Small curve of leather that rode
on his backside in the pickup
to auctions every Tuesday,

that stretched and marked
the right pocket of his Levis,
that padded the wood chairs

of the café where he gossiped
with the other farmers about
grain yields, corn futures,

that rests now in the cupboard
above the sewing machine
where Mother put it after

she cleared away his fifteen
trim suits, his thirty shirts,
his pajamas and robe, his neat

row of shoes. His pickup
sits undriven in the left bay
of the garage. Only the wallet

remains, packed, as he left it,
with plastic cards, photo IDs,
gold membership numbers,

the unspent fifty dollars
and the unused lines of credit
we all hope will someday

save us. At the Prairie Nights
Casino we plug the slots
for him, for the big lotto payoff,

waiting for his always
earthly luck to rub off on us.
But everything comes up lemons

and oranges, flags, rubies,
and diamonds, in the wrong
combinations—the mixed bag

of fruit and wild cards
that never fell into place the way
we'd always hoped or imagined.

Usual Magic

Remember rooster, that cock,
with his deep blue, oil-in-water
feathers? How he envied our gold

and yellow making. Mornings,
he hated the weakest chick.
Afternoons, he loathed

the strongest. At night
he tucked his bruised comb under
his pinfeathers, and secretly despised

the rest. Even Mary Jane Bitz,
our sister's friend, with her sleek black
ponytail and her midnight blue racer.

He hopped on the metal runner
as she pedaled our gravel drive,
and pecked her on the back,

saying, *Get out, get out, get out
of my yard, no one makes anything
here without me.* It wasn't sad

when mother had to take him
to the stump. The next day
the sun rose and rose again

without his awful noise,
and the small round wonders
appeared in the straw beds

by their usual magic.

Annie K and the Function of Y

Under the half moon of her glasses
and the radiator's disapproving hiss,
under the silent footfall behind us,

we crunched numbers, calculated
coefficients. We called her Annie K
behind her hammy back, Mrs. Leier

or nothing to her face. Her wool suits
were iron-chested, World War Two,
double-breasted. Her cinched-in

waist vexed and fretted, the hour
we spent in math each day with her.
On the slippery pyramid of her

formulations, I was failing, failing,
falling down the architectonic steps
of her equations. The unknowns

were like Catholic gods to me,
sequestered in heaven, and speaking
only Latin. She fussed over the brainy

boys, backtracked if they faltered.
Her eyes extrapolated my short list
of variables—my hands would work

the stove, the plow, the milker,
my pen confined to thank you notes,
to-do lists. *Never marry a man*

in your own profession, she said
one day to the ceiling (the only lesson
I took from calculus). The squish

and wobble of her shoes unnerved us,
those stamped-down, high-heel patrols.
We bent our heads, speculated the value

of y to the worried whisper of erasers.
We scrutinized the inscrutable cosine
to the rustle and swish of her girdle,

factoring the unknowns lurking
beneath her skirts. And the spider web
ganglion of leg hair, trapped and

matted under her support hose,
was final proof to us of what
she thought inconsequential

and of no significance whatsoever.

Thinning the Litter

The fourth daughter out of five children,
the youngest girl, worries, her whole life,

about the litter of kittens, afraid to take
the last piece of bread after watching

the strong wrestle the milky teat from
the weak. The fourth daughter, afraid

to take the last piece of pizza, the last
kernels of corn, scoop them up in one

clean swipe, stubborn mouth refusing
to eat or speak. The fourth daughter

out of five children on the farm, forced
to thin the litter, to choose the survivors—

the white one, the black one, the star-marked
one—understanding the signs of favor,

the signs of disfavor. The fourth daughter
out of five children on a farm takes

the brown burlap bag, the brick,
takes the knocks on the side of the barn.

The Hardness of Math

Grade school dance.
Too much patent leather

and the slither of slips
under cotton dresses.

Cafeteria tables stacked
into corners, and streamers

twisting from rafters.
In the air, the mix

of floor wax and peanut butter,
as a boy and a girl dance toe

to toe, talking about the hardness
of math. The record player

spinning 45s as the boy
and girl dance hip bone

to hip bone, the small
beginning of something

rising between them.

Older Sister

Forever, she rides
in front of me
on the school bus,
a lime-green mohair
draped over pale
shoulders, her stiff
auburn flip bouncing
firmly. In the curved
mirror of the mahogany
dressing table, she teases,
rats, and sprays her hair
into submission. Year
after year, her class photos
reflect magazine-rack
knowledge of the properly
curving eyebrow,
the correct application
of blush to the cheek.
No sweaty backseats
on her conscience,
no cigarettes in her
drawers. The older sister
wore bras that fit
and skirts that hugged
the knee. The older sister
never used one more
chocolate chip
than the recipe required.

Hurricane

When hurricane rolls into town,
her wide-bottomed Ford blowing
blue plumes of diesel, her muffler
scraping sparks, the barometer rises

twelve degrees. The weatherman
develops a twitch in his neck.
When Judy hits town, her billfold
wadded with cash, headed for

the wide-open space of the mall,
she leaves her Ford parked at a crazy
angle across the yellow grid.
At the peanut bar, over the foam

of a Big Top beer she yanks
an accordion of photos from
her purse, the five children
she raised *without that asshole,*

perfect teeth, perfect skin, perfect
ACTs, the youngest, a single cell
split perfectly from her body.
What can this woman not make

from the nothing that was given
to her. In the morning, she pops
a Diet Coke, torches a Marlboro,
inhales her usual breakfast.

In the early light, I watch
the curtain blow behind her,
the smoke curling in tendrils
through her hair. In the Bible,

Judith is dangerous, only allowed
in the Apocrypha, and Deborah
is the singer of songs, the leader
of troops into battle. Oh, the plans

our mother had when she named us.
In school, they called her *twee-twunk*,
because of her thunder thighs,
and her unpronounceable *R*s.

This morning, I want to call her
by her rightful name—bear-woman,
force-of-nature, sister. This morning,
I want to call her sister

From the Desk of Them

The gals share a private joke with the world
and their tired husbands. They go on long trips

alone, or with other gals. Taking their lunch
downtown, they plan church cookbooks,

tell the waiter dirty jokes, laugh and pretend
to blush. Throwing their diamond-ringed

fingers up in public, they fan their faces
with their napkins and say, *is it hot in here*

or is it me? They enjoy sex, we know,
and are responsible for sending out all

high school reunion letters. Later in life,
they move into interior design, wear chic

crepe dresses, have maids and secretaries,
and stationery, which is from the desk of them.

Hearing My Mother's Voice

The blinking light tells me
to unwind the tape, let loose

the voices that have called me.
I unbutton my blouse, pull on

a sweatshirt. Time to let go
of the meetings, the commute,

what my boss said in passing.
I recognize her even from

the other room, anxious breath
on the line, the ends of words

clamped tight. Her voice rises
at the end of each sentence,

as if forever asking. The one time
she visited, she quizzed me again

and again, *Now, to get back on
the freeway, do I go right and follow*

*the loop, or go under the highway
and turn left?* In her small town

there's not even a yellow light
flashing caution. Beside the phone,

now I rewind the tape, listen again
for the details, the heavy breath,

the vowels that refuse to sing. But I find
it's me, calling home earlier in the day

reminding whoever gets this message
to pick up some bread, some milk,

and asking, in a small voice,
what we will be doing tonight.

After We Make Love, the Phone Rings

He pulls the receiver
across the white sheets.
I study the hollows
of his cheeks, so deep
in the half light.

The silence becomes
the voice of his mother
returning his call.
What does he want,
she asks. Her words,

a small buzzing in
his ear. Nothing,
he says, falling back,
a solid thump
on the sheets,

the dark cord
glistening in a curl
up his abdomen.
*Just thought
I'd let you know,*

he twirls the cord
on his fingers,
*that I won't
be home for dinner.*
And they laugh

that easy laugh
between them.
It's funny because
he's a moved-away son,
and hasn't eaten

at home for years.

More Like Hunger

Oh peach, let me rest for a time
beneath the sway of your branches.

Tell me again about the fever
of your childhood, the gold teeth

of your youth. Then shall we
join hands and recount the many

differences between us. I've come,
exhausted, from a world marked

by your arrivals, full of rooms
made too large and luminous

by your absence. In the great
maw of days, I struggle to recall

the rumble of your voice moving
through empty rooms like thunder,

no, more like hunger. Once I believed
the world would drop with succulence

in my lap. So long ago fallen, I lie
in this bed, heavy with sweetness,

imagining the swell and curve
of you. Listen, inside each of us

is a hard pit that wants to be stripped
free. And underneath, a grainy hollow

with deep grooves and wild unbroken
threads, never before seen

longing to be licked clean.

Alchemy

*Just because all of our computers aren't put in a row
doesn't mean they're not an assembly line.*
—Nancy Reinecke

It's hard, this business
of turning straw into gold.
Every day someone's coming

to your door, saying, *Gimme
gimme, gimme what you got,*
and you turn over these soft

round kernels, spun fresh
from the smooth yolk
of your body. They slip

them deep in their pockets,
calculating the value
per gram, what the market

will allow. People agree
that nothing is ever lost,
only changed to other forms.

This glowing humming
inside you is the reason
you're confined to mining

the day's details down
to something pulsing
and new. It's a mystery

why you stay. See, others
are running in the moonlight,
shouting, *Lovers, bring me more*

lovers. You watch them from
the balcony, your breath
rising and falling, throwing words,

throwing curses to the vacancies,
your hands moving in strange,
unaccountable ways. Busy again,

at making something
out of what other people thought
was nothing.

Fish While You Can

—for Mark Vinz

Let's not end up like our man,
Alfie, in the nursing home
messing his pants and raving
about metal lures and tangled lines.
As the nurses turn him to change
his soiled sheets, he's pulling in
the big one. Careful, he yells
at the attendant, his arms caught
in casting pose. *Hold on to him
now. Hold on.* Dark is the body
of water below him, the lake turns
to river turns to sea. Each year
we write letters to each other
about the poems we know
will get away until next summer
or better weather. I want
a moment each day like the one
I saw in a movie—two kids sitting
in a magical boat in the middle
of an enchanted lake
as rainbow-skinned trout leap
in wide arcs into their arms.
Why do we settle, each year
for tin cans and bottom feeders,
for poems like old boots,
their drunk tongues refusing
to speak. Listen, something
waits for us. The lake turns
to river turns to sea. Careful now,
easy with the line. *Easy.*
Ah man, she's a beauty.

May All Our Children Swim

—Family Reunion, Holiday Inn

Could it be the grandparents who watch us?
The unbroken line of six Josephs, the Marys
and Barbaras who spread their bones from

the steppes to the plains, rising in a silent
column behind us. They who were broken
as they broke the land so that we might

vacation in this state of ten thousand lakes.
In turn, we hover in the balcony
like squatters, overlooking our children

who swim in the kidney-shaped pool.
Feeling one generation away from
poolside, we sit in vacation clothes,

crisp from their packages. We shuffle
our creamy white feet in unfamiliar
sandals and throw caution like life

preservers over the railing—*Don't forget*
your earplugs. Stay out of the deep end.
Born too soon for city pools, destined

to work hardscrabble, we worry about
our swimming children, if one of them
goes down, who among us could save

a drowning child? Below, the true citizens,
barefoot and swaddled in fluffy robes,
lounge and drink poolside. Snapping

their fingers for waiters in bow ties
who bend to deliver trays of appetizers,
cold beers, room tabs to sign. The class

of '65 is here, the marquee
confirms—a thirty-year reunion.
The two girls voted best personality

and class clown, dressed in draping black
stand on the edge of the deep end.
They shed their big gold shoes, plug

their noses, hold hands and plunge
in a large splashing roll. They surface
with a giant roar that explodes

to the rafters, reaching us in the balcony,
our faces drawn with worry as we watch
our youngest, small and pink—our little

peanut floating along with the big kids,
a green rubber turtle ringing her waist.
Confident of her equipment, she holds

her nose, throws her body back and kicks
in a wild dog paddle. She works at this,
for hours, her tongue bent with

determination, as we watch amazed
at how easily she rises, her body breaking
the plane again and again. Who knows

what the grandparents make of this?
Imagine—our young, floating along,
so buoyant on the untroubled surface.

This New Quiet

Wearing Dead Women's Clothes

Remember the Mormon thrift store
in Idaho, as big and tidy as a K-mart,
where Wanda rifled through the racks

and found me a seal skin coat
that was practically new, and warm
as the French Riviera. We'd run

headlong into the cold wild west
with nothing but our little black
dresses, good for shaking tail

and singing doo-wop. I was colder
than Canada. How I wanted
that dark fur around me but I worried

about the baby seals. I'd seen it on TV—
bearded men with clubs waiting
on beaches in places as remote

as Newfoundland. Wearing fur,
I said, creates a market. Honey,
she said, her voice rising an octave,

her curved fingernails, long and sharp
as harpoons, that's the advantage
of wearing dead women's clothes.

They take all that bad karma
with them when they go. I still have
the sweatshirt she gave me in Ames

when I was sick and all the clothes
in my suitcase were spandex
and leather and sweated clean through.

In the motel room, she peeled
the layers from me and swabbed
my body cool with a cloth. I lay

panting on the damp sheets
like something stripped clean
and brand new. Wanda,

I blubbered before the pills
knocked me out, my problem
is that I wasn't properly mothered.

And then I fell silent, lost
my voice and couldn't sing
for days. I was useful to no one,

but she came back. Every day
I heard humming as she unlatched
the door, her voice breaking

clean like waves through the room.
Mmm, mmm, mmm, she sang,
checking my temperature,

furiously shaking the mercury
to the bottom, and, Sister,
she whispered, when she thought

I was beyond hearing,
when you going to get up
and give a rat's ass.

Our Common Friend

Although it was years ago and she
was a friend of a friend, I recall
her name was Pam. I've forgotten

our common friend's name,
but I remember so well the story
she told about a hot tub party

where Pam (this was in the seventies)
was pursued in the public waters—
lights turned low and guitars blaring

on the stereo. And under the warm
swirling wet, Pam entertained,
the interests of a bass player

from a local metal band whose habit,
we all observed, was to lure women
in the crowd to him by stroking

his greased black moustache
(this was in the seventies), swaying
his tight-crotch hips, and angling,

just so, a reflective mirror pick-guard
he'd installed on his Fender
precision bass so the spotlight

threw a sharp beam—arcing a triangle
of light from the spot cam
to the pickguard and into the eyes

of the chosen woman, now blinded
and unable to flee (just as certain
animals stun their prey). That night

Pam drew his attention in the hot tub,
by training her arsenal on him.
(We all admired her iron points,

round and pruned brown,
next to our small tawny circles.)
Which gave rise to a moment later

in the cabana—small triangles
of jungle print stripped away,
the ceramic tile, cold and grainy

beneath them. And in the grit
and the growl, he begged her
(she told us later) pleaded for her

to take him home, to soft lights,
to cotton sheets. We all admired
how she silenced his whimpers—

Not here, not like this—forcing him
to bring the jewels into the harsh
public light. Here was our champion,

a woman with breasts like battalions
and a locker room tongue. She,
who is married now, I'm certain,

with a house on a tree-lined street,
kids in college, a self-cleaning oven,
disconnected from this story

as I am from our common friend,
forgotten as we've all become so late
in this century, even from ourselves.

Dylan's Lost Years

Somewhere between Hibbing
and New York, the red rust streets
of the iron range and the shipping yards
of the Atlantic, somewhere between

Zimmerman and Dylan was a pit stop
in Fargo, a superman-in-the-phone-booth
interlude, recalled by no one but
the Danforth Brothers who hired

the young musician, fresh in town
with his beat-up six string and his
small town twang, to play shake,
rattle, and roll, to play good golly,

along with Wayne on keys and Dirk
on bass, two musical brothers
whom you might still find playing
the baby grand, happy hours

at the southside Holiday Inn.
And if you slip the snifter a five,
Wayne might talk, between how high
the moon, and embraceable you, about

Dylan's lost years, about the Elvis sneer,
the James-Dean leather collar pulled
tight around his neck, about the late night
motorcycle rides, kicking over the city's

garbage cans. And how they finally
had to let him go, seeing how he was
more trouble than he was worth,
and with everyone in full agreement

that the new boy just could not sing.

Mooch

　　　　　When Mooch shows up
at your door, he's carrying that midnight blue,

hard-backed suitcase that his mother got
when she went away to college, the kind

Doris Day pulled out of the closet and never
got fully packed when she became emotional

and decided to run away from Rock Hudson.
In the movie, Rock rushes in and fixes things.

In your real life, Mooch steps in and never
leaves. He lives out of that suitcase. Everything

but his guitars fit between its clever latches—
two pair of pants, four shirts, and five unmatched

pairs of socks. No underwear, because he doesn't
wear them, and no toothbrush, thank you,

he will just use yours. Isn't it handy how
the case fits under your bed, leaving no trace

of him, except for the constant hand on the remote,
the skinny bottom planted on your couch,

and, oh, how he prides himself for only eating
leftovers out of your crowded refrigerator.

Joe Mohlers Wanted To Be

a drummer. His mother kept
a dusty museum of his progress—
the sticks and snare drum heads

that crumbled in his hands,
the self-destructing trap sets.
He liked to eat crunchy foods

close to your ear and read
the newspaper over your back,
whispering disaster into your ears.

He'd settle back on the old green couch
and inhale pot like regular tobacco,
yawning and blowing smoke rings.

He wore paisley shirts, and those
brown suede shoes you can buy
on sale at Payless any time of the year.

On the road he learned the art
of whoring around, eventually
overcoming the compulsion

to marry every woman he slept with.
What could we do, he owned half
the P.A. and the yellow van we drove

to gigs in. The day we fired him
it was only because, no matter
how much Joe Mohlers wanted to be

a drummer—with his tweed hat,
and his knotted red neckerchief—
he remained absolutely devoid

of any ability to keep a beat, which,
above all other possible charms,
every good drummer must have.

Big Guitar Sound

Although everyone told Randy
he'd have to go to Spain
to get the truly big guitar sound

the kind that comes barreling
out of the guitar like the bulls
out of the gates at Pamplona,

he thought he'd try Des Moines first
a place called Last Chance Guitars
famous for having refused Dylan

use of the bathroom one time back
in the eighties during his Jesus-phase
when he really had to go, but the clerk

didn't recognize the pout behind
the sunglasses that curved, dark
and mirrored around his famous face.

Everything about Randy was oversized—
massive hambone hands, long strike-a-pose
legs, big hair threatening to topple him

as he bent to play a lick, his tongue out
dreaming of finding a sound as thick
as cream off a spout. At the Last Chance

he found the metal zone, a row of pedals,
all strung together, LEDs popping on
and off like Christmas lights, the flanger

that doubled his tone, made him two
instead of one, still sounding less
than a trip to Spain—the good

that breathing in the air would do.
He tried the baby tremolo, pulsating
through the neck of his guitar. He shook

the life from it, stomping on the chorus,
a thick, shimmering sound rising.
The wah, wah, the super fuzz,

the hyper turbo overdrive grunge
phase shifter that made him sound
like thirteen chain saws gnawing

through walls, a continent away
from Memphis and still not as big
as if he'd gone to Spain.

Do Drop Inn

When they found Keith
in a motel room in Jacksonville,
someone said, they had to break
the chain, throw a shoulder against

the dark splinter of wood, force
the metal rings to give up
the mounted gold clasp.
Someone else said the links

were swinging free and the police
walked into an already open
door. Doesn't matter except
to know he wasn't alone

in the end. Jacksonville's hot
this time of year. Keith would've
hated going in a mom-and-pop
do drop inn with a marquee

flashing, *eat, sleep, bowl.*
Those hands could play
the three-over-four, the slide,
the strut, the syncopation,

like nobody could teach. He
was always going to California,
but first the dirty dancehalls,
then the pregnant wife,

after that the fat paychecks
on the cocktail circuit
held him, always in debt,
but on the way out and going

to California shortly thereafter.
When I met him, I had a habit
of quitting smoking for twenty
minutes, and he would vow

to leave his wife. In that room
where they found him,
I imagine a woman slip
out from under and collect

her clothes. She slides
the chain free and runs down
the hallway, falling apart as
she runs, falling apart as she runs

away from Keith and the way
he knew how to play.

The Day Montana Turned

The day Montana turned into a movie was bleak,
    overcast, a silent, windless day of people, moving
        through intersections, all morning, crossing over

but never once colliding. I wore sunglasses,
    behind charcoal-tinted windows in the black van,
        angle parked on Third Street as he took his wounded

keyboard, into the repair shop. So, maybe I did empty
    a glass of orange juice into its guts the night before,
        and maybe not-so-accidentally. He and everything

in my sight belonged to his wife, or so she informed me
    over her crystal phone, comfortable back home
        with her Audi and her fox terriers. When the cool

juice hit the hot wires, maybe I did enjoy the slight
    crackling sound, the burnt wire smell, and the tiny
        blue plume that rose from the circuits like a minor

explosion. Everything's expensive, I hissed into his ear
    as he bent to eye the catastrophe. And maybe
        that's why he slugged me extra hard that night

as I soaked in the bathtub, my body slippery from soap,
    scrubbing the layers of salt that settled like a fine grain
        under my skin. So the next morning, we went

downtown to see what could be done for the machine,
    and I sat in the truck wearing sunglasses to cover the explosion
        of orange to red to maroon that was blossoming

on my face. On the street, people moved through
    intersections like sleepwalkers, never once colliding.
        Their faces, covered with mufflers, chuffed cold smoke

into the air, like clouds in need of dialogue. I tried to read,
    their breath, but there were no words. It was not cartoon,
        it was movie, reeling silently by, as I sat in the van unable

to step out, afraid to be lost without even this nothing that was left to me.

Turning to Herself

She doubts the succession
of circles, the deep grooves,
like stories within stories

that the garbled reflection
of the rest area mirror tells.
The lines rim her eyes adding up

to zero, for she cannot recall
when this roadmap gathered
on her face. The sleep of years

upon her, she trips from
the van into this late night
rest stop, hungry for candy

and relief, stalled out on
the porcelain tiles, the flush
and flushing from the cold

row of stalls. The dim light
tells a story of smooth, unbroken
flight, gliding unobstructed

along surfaces, all leading
to this catalogue of travel,
this book whose spine

she's never cracked. The circles
show movement, like rings
inside the trunk, revealing

what the surface conceals—
the dry years, the criss-crosses,
the circle backs, the pockmarks—

all signs of terrain traveled
but not recalled. Turning to
herself she puts her hands

to her face, as if touching
Braille, turning to herself
she reads her own story

for the first time.

This New Quiet

The day after the fire, all their equipment
charred in a ditch and blown to ashes,
the thin axle of the truck lying on its side

like the burnt-out frame of a dragonfly,
they gathered in a circle of old couches,
most of them sitting forward, their eyes

studying the swirls in the worn carpet.
They who had the power to make
so much noise sat in this new quiet.

In voices ringing flat as the many roads
they'd traveled, they tried out the new
words the fire left on their tongues.

They did not speak of debt or creditors,
nor did they speak of lost guitars—the blonde
Les Paul, and the rosewood Gibson double-neck

that sang sweetly in its velvet case
as it rolled down the highway. They sat
in silence. Outside traffic rushed by,

the drone and clatter of passing trains,
the honk of angry horns as the sun dialed
around the room, angling a view through

the windows. Finally, someone stood.
It was the tall blonde guitar player
who rose, wobbly in his black boots.

He stood in the center of the spiral,
raised his thin hands to his face and
blew out one long exhale. It hissed

through the room like a wild balloon
losing steam. When all the wind was
out of him, he gulped one deep breath,

swung a long arm like a knockout punch
through the sheer emptiness of air,
and said, *Fuck*. It was only

one word. It was inadequate
for the moment. But it was
a good place to start.

The Way of Fire

Every year you give your mother
candles for Christmas. You buy her
brass nightlamps, pewter votives,

marble hurricane lamps. Every year
you watch her pick through the package,
lift the thing into the air. Lovely,

she says and finds a place on one of her
cool, clean surfaces. How to explain
this distance you have come

so far from the tow of her waters.
How to introduce this other mother
who has left you disinherited, licked you

clean with her violent tongue. Every year
you return to unlit wicks, still white,
pressed neatly into the smooth tips

of tapers. Even on these holidays
of eggnog and sitting in circles,
all your gifts unused. She's worried

about wax drippings, and burn holes
and whether or not the drapery
will catch. Besides, what is it good for,

she asks, when we have light already?

Palimpsest

You are here.
—Notation on Concourse Maps

Let Y be your destination, the unnamed
place beyond the flickering fluorescence
of corridors, the terrazzo floors worn smooth

from the shoes of the dead. Let X be
your present location, the uncharted
space between pencil and chalk marks,

the keypad's incessant clatter. Listen,
you are here, a blip on a screen, transfixed
between home and away. It is possible

to create a life, doors opening to other
doors, the fresh breeze of tomorrow
rushing in to make the world new

each day. The canvas remembers
its maker, inside the hairline grooves
under the brushstrokes live the barest

traces—whispered thoughts, words
spoken, mundane as groceries, bills
and gasoline. The fingerprints

of the dead are everywhere, the tiny
whorls like plots to cities where one
could spend a life. Best to find

your own path, chart the roadmap
etched under your skin, sit down,
get to know the wantings of your feet.

On the Corner of Hunger and Thirst

I've read about the all-consuming ferocious love
of the original parents who gazed upon their young

with such relish and delight that all they could think
to do was eat them. And this is when, the story goes,

god took down his work papers, touched his pencil
to his tongue, and reduced by forty percent the intensity

of parental love. Still I've felt this way about kittens,
that awful crush of love, wanting to squeeze them

to death in their cuteness. And I've seen husbands
wriggle from the grip of love's terrible claw. Oh, rare friend,

brother, I was after something exquisite that would break
with taste on my tongue those afternoons we talked,

the light outside turning from blue to sapphire to deep
indigo, my lips pressed close to your ear whispering

our words into stillness. I was after that mix of salt
and blood between us, something more than this dry

paper life, the feel of gristle on our tongues
like the swish of whiskey and sirloin late at night

after everyone who doesn't know how to party
has left the party. Once I ate a cheeseburger

with raw onions and mayonnaise so sublime,
I have searched for it ever since that night, tripping

on chocolate mesc when Dave Eggen found me
jammed into a phone booth on Hwy 3,

a halo of hungry moths circling the ghostly globe.
I was pumping dimes into the slot, trying to win

that big, communications lotto, my fingers hallucinating
their way into sleeping bedrooms, darkened kitchens

where wives in curlers, husbands in torn underwear
rose to hear me rave about the absolute transforming

power of the latest southern shipment. That's when
Dave Eggen folded me into his Fury and drove to

the cafe where he knew to order me the #6
that sizzled wise and inscrutable in its bed of fries,

just as you arrived, your voice coming over the line
in twists and turns, digressions and variations, oh

sweet five by five, we extemporized there
where we met on the corner of hunger and thirst.

Me, with my flask of buried teas, and you with your
sweet bits of jerky, remember, back in the day

when we were all ears, eyes and hands for each other.

Everything's a Verb | 1995

To Peter
and
for Lydia

Truly, we writers are the secretaries of death.
  —John Berger

Places Only the Body Knows

Speaking the Language

Again the language fails me
trying to describe her.
Words fragment on my tongue.
Vowels roll into tomatoes
ripening on her windowsill.
Consonants clatter and stack
neatly in her cupboard.

She taught me to speak
this language. She said,
I am very exciting, meaning
she was looking forward
to something. She said, *bodado*,
that small white vegetable
she peeled each day, her hand
riding high on the blade
of a paring knife, her fingers
permanently bent to the shape
of a medium-sized potato.

She said, *uppsie daisy*,
pulling me to her large
round bosom long after
I was too heavy to lift.
She said, *That was good, not?*
meaning, Don't you think so?

How do I decipher
this language she left me.
These recipes for knephla
and strudel that never include
flour—flour being the ingredient

too obvious for her to mention.
These recipes that do not tell
how many minutes to bake
or at what temperature.

Lost to me, all of it,
like the magnet earrings
she promised
out of her jewelry box
that were baubles in front,
and magnets in back,
that did not pierce
or clip, that held
the earring to the lobe
by some rare, invisible power.

When the Names Still Fit the Faces

On a shelf in the back of the big closet
after her death we found stacks and stacks

of photo albums full of her subjects. How many
did she fool with her stammering *just-a-second*,

her fiddling, *this darn thing*, her eye stalling
for the perfect cinematic moment, that infinity

of seconds when genuine smiles stretch thin
and elastic, when loose arms thrown casually

over shoulders grow heavy. The early photos
feature plain women in fancy dresses and new cars

parked by old houses. The later photos are thick
with nyloned thighs, Christmas trees dripping

with ornaments, uncles long dead and children
long grown old. Surely, this is the trail

she would have us follow, back to the people
we would never know, the selves we would never

recall, back to the time when the names
still fit the faces. In the end fearing loss

of memory she took to labeling every photo,
putting the name, finally, to the image,

sprawling *Ed* across Ed's blank forehead,
tracing *Reinhold* on a high, thin, cheekbone,

spiraling *Emma* up Emma's bleach-blonde
beehive. She, the hand behind the shutter

is seldom pictured. Only in rare moments
when someone has seized the camera

and forced her into the frame
does she appear—grinning, big-boned,

and out of context—with a large *Me*
emblazoned across her bosom.

Behave

On TV when the cops crash
through your door they scream,
Stop, or I'll shoot, but I recall
a newly minted deputy
storming our kegger years ago.
Fingers itchy for the stiff leather
of his holster, he made for
the bonfire yelling, Shoot,
or I'll stop. Such things

stay with you, like the way
my ex used to say, Now you
just behave, when he thought
my neck had slipped too far
out of the loop of his noose.
I'd curl my legs under me,
and purr, Oh sure, honey,
I'm *being-have*, pronouncing it
with a slight southern accent,
a word like a silk sheet
slipping, perfectly,
off my tongue. But you know

how it is with cats, all sweetness
curled on the couch
when you're home,
but shredding their nails
on the chiffon as your car
backs down the driveway.
Don't kid yourself,
they're looming large
over the gerbil and pissing
wild arcs into the flowerpot,
even as your garage door
yawns to its slow mechanical
close. Lately I've been thinking
about the word, *behave*,
how it's made entirely of verbs,
but it's all about going nowhere.

Being-have means, *being had*,
means, *having been*, means,
being a has-been. It reminds me

of the way I could never breathe,
when I was a kid, that long, slow
hyperventilating experience
of childhood. I'd go white and claw
my neck. My sisters would turn
and groan, Dad, she's doing it

again. And Dad would get
his red face right next to mine,
hunker down as if to adjust
the TV, and scream, *Now you
just relax!* Sure, the air of fear

rushed greedily into my lungs.
But even though they all believed
it had worked, I always knew
it hadn't.

Wormwood

My father tells the story
he has told every day of his life,
of the woman brought from the south

where they still practiced the old ways,
when Doc Simon said there was no hope
because fluid was in both of his young lungs,

how the uncles fetched her by carriage
on the shortest day of winter,
how she dug deep under tall banks

for wormwood, a grayish-greenish
stinky weed that no one, not even
the herefords would eat, how she

boiled milk and dropped the leaves
in, how she made a bitter soup
for him to drink. Here my father

sits back and breathes deep
wormwood's tale—little leaf,
tiny slip, smuggled through customs

years ago inside some washerwoman's
sleeve. He has reached the border
of what he knows. What lies beyond

is unknown country, a tangled
wilderness of sheets, soaked
with sweat, cold rags pressed

to a burning forehead, prayers,
whispering over him in the night.
Beyond this point lives gossip,

hearsay, the places only the body
knows. Here my father's hands
grow wings, as if forming the story

from air, the old blue veins tracing
the slow curve of memory. *They say*
she named the fever "little fire"

and warned it to find a better place
to burn. When lost, he invents details—
the dozen eggs she took in payment

for her work—but he always keeps
the ending the same. How Doc Simon
asked about him, some weeks later

not seeing a notice of death
in the news. How Grandpa said,
Wormwood. How Doc Simon said,

That could have killed him.

And Who Do You Belong To?

Even in my ghost costume
I'm recognizable,
with my three older sisters
the nun, the witch and
the pirate, who are only in it
for the candy, and my brother,
who believes he is Napoleon.

It's not the question,
*And what are you supposed
to be?* that bothers me.
Under my clean, white sheet,
it's apparent, I'm a ghost.
It's the other question,
And who do you belong to?
that sets our feet shuffling.
Our answer, like a chicken bone,
we hold in our throats
considering treachery,
until finally, the nun
spits it out, our father's
name. And that is when

the wife calls the husband
off the couch, the dog
comes too, and even the parrot
takes note, it's Felix's kids
at their front door mercy.
We are the children
of the year-round trickster.
Felix, who pokes every chest
for the invisible stain. Felix of
I got your nose, I got your nose

fame. And tonight we go
door-to-door, forced to
wait out the good laugh.

And I begin to cry,
I'm so tired of people laughing,
and I cry straight through to
the St. Philip Neri party
when the Sisters ask,
*how many jelly beans
in this jar?* I get weepy then

because I only know up to ten,
so my sister, the pirate,
guesses for me, writing down
one number less
than her own guess,
and I end up winning
the whole goddamn jar.

The Permanent

The wind that blew me from the porch
that afternoon came out of the dusty nowhere

that is the high plains. My mother, inside,
winding Grandma's fine feathers into pink,

permanent rollers, did not see the rock
that knocked a hole in my skull,

could not stop to watch the blood
rush from the wound, only heard the wail

wind up, the siren song that blew long after
the gush had stopped, long after the rush

of water and my sisters' shampooing hands
had washed it all away. Mother applied

the permanent solution, guaranteeing
Grandma's curls were now a matter of record.

The skunky smell of permanent drifted
from the kitchen, the rotten egg odor permeated

all the rooms. Grandma took me to her lap,
that great lost continent of thigh. Let me see,

she said, tilting my cracked egg head
to the side. Oy, yoy, yoy, she clicked

her tongue with regret. *Oy, yoy, yoy.*
That's going to be permanent.

Motorcade

From here it becomes necessary
to ship all bodies east.
—Thomas McGrath

I was seven when it happened
in the second grade, but old enough
to know it was serious
when Sister Jacinta, bleary-eyed
and wrinkled, announced
that our Catholic president
had been shot. We rose,
hands over our hearts to say
the Pledge-Allegiance, then hands
together to pray the Our-Father
although, I believe, all along,
we understood we were praying
for the soul and not the man.

What I remember most is Ronnie Bissell
sneezing through everything.
A tin of pepper on his desk,
for what I don't recall
perhaps show-and-tell,
but some dark itching powder
had gotten into his nose.
And somehow I've always known
that he enjoyed it,
the body betraying itself
at that very solemn moment.
He was the flamboyant one,
class clown, moved away
after graduation, like all of us.
I never heard from him again
until last year when I saw
his obituary in the paper:
still single, his address
listed as San Francisco. Bodies
are flowing back to us from places
less parochial. How immune

we believed ourselves to be
so far from the swirling locus
of events. There are moments
like these in history
that hold themselves up
like great roaring surfaces,
too large to reveal anything,
but that one single frame
from the movie
of our own lives. That night,

we watched it on the news:
the motorcade running the gauntlet.
President Kennedy alive and smiling
then dead, alive and smiling,
then dead. Jackie in her pillbox hat
and short waist-coat, crawling
onto the trunk of the convertible,
almost reaching the arms
of the secret service man, almost
going backward for one long moment,

while all else rushed forward,
then thinking better
and returning to the back seat,
to her already dead husband,
the motorcade picking up speed
and accelerating madly
out of view of the camera.

I am Upstairs, Trying to Be Quiet

when i think of her, i think of silence,
my mouth growing tight across my face
after she has told me not to sing
in the house, not to move around so much,
told me she could fix dinner twice
in the time it would take to show me once,
what i would only forget
and have to be shown again anyway,
and how i would only make a mess
that she would have to clean up later.
i hear a cupboard door slam.
she is in the kitchen with father,
talking about lazy kids.
i am upstairs, trying to be quiet.
even though i'm safe in my room
with the door shut, i know she
can still hear me breathing.
often now when i dream,
i dream of that place. things
follow me there i cannot stop—
street gangs, rock bands, nazis.
it's different every time. i hear them
downstairs, trashing the furniture,
raiding the refrigerator and leaving
their scraps on the kitchen table.
they are playing the stereo loud
and having their women in her bedroom.
i want to stop them, but there's nothing
i can do. the sounds come to me
like hard fists in my sleep. i am upstairs,
trying to be quiet. downstairs,
they are tearing her limb from limb.

Birthmark

It has been seventy-two hours
since he last slept. I have been

counting. He has rummaged
through the drawers, muttering

to himself. He has threatened the lives
of all the major appliances.

It has been seventy-two hours
and now he is asleep. The room

is like a vault when I go upstairs
to check. The air is stale.

The curtains drawn.
In this big bed, he is nothing more

than a spill of black hair, the tension
of his jaw let loose, the beacon

in his forehead extinguished.
I check his heart first

then his covers. He is overheated.
All over his skin is damp

and rosy. I touch the white
streak in his hair, a birthmark

from the tongs where the doctors
tried to extract him

from his mother. Born with a black
eye on Friday the thirteenth,

he came out fighting, he said,
because he didn't want to come out

at all. The garbage man
is outside with his clanking cans

and backup bell. I cover
his ears and he wraps himself

around me. I cover his ears
and he wraps himself around

the wideness of my hips.

Between Wives

I was trying to teach him a lesson
    that day she stepped in
with her wide skirts, her sing-song
    assurances. I was trying to kill

the thing in him that was killing me.
    At the Village Inn, she and I
are having one of those civil discussions
    women have after everything›s over.

He's at home, fuming through
    half-packed rooms as we drain cup
after cup over the subject of him. Listen,
    I say, quoting Heinemann, a curious thing

has happened to our generation of men.
    There were the guys that went to Vietnam,
and the guys that, for whatever reason,
    did not go. I tell her this because

she's too young to know. Your eyes,
    she says, are the most amazing green.
She is like this: all lies and diversions.
    My eyes are the harsh lens he has seen

himself through for seven years. Love,
    I say, pouring my tenth cup, love is like
a ferris wheel. Sometimes the damn thing
    creaks to a halt and, if you're on bottom

you have the option of getting off. Her eyes
    are clear blue, tears welling up
as she says, let me know if you want back on,
    because I will get out of the way

for you. If I wanted you out of the way,
    I say, lifting a finger, I would move you.
But it's all smoke I'm blowing.
    I am the second wife; soon she will be

the third, and I will be the nightmare
        he had between wives. The waiter
appears, all concern. He checks
        the thermos and slides the bill

perfectly between us. What if
        I told you, she says, reaching across
the table, that your precious wheel
        has started up without you. Sister,

I think, oh sister,
        how I want to kiss you full
on those lips he loves and let loose
        this thing that rattles

in my chest. *Remember to keep*
        the angle of your vision wide
when he comes swinging, I want to say,
        but I swallow these words

like a bad meal and retreat to the wisdom
        of experts. According to Heinemann,
I offer, like one who has read
        an informative news report on the subject,

a split has erupted in our generation
        of men. A dialogue has yet to occur
between them. Try to remember that, I say,
        that is the killing thing about him.

He Will Make Some Woman

A trail of wringing hands
leading back to mother
follows him. He will make

some woman forget
biological timeclocks,
cling to spare moments

before motocross,
parachutes, and third worlds
claim him. Willingly,

he will go, gearing up
and slapping backs
all the way. He'll stand

in open ground during air raids,
turn over poker tables
in hot, smoky rooms.

Like Burt Lancaster
in *From Here to Eternity*,
he'll jump into street brawls,

kicking the knife
out of Fatso's hand,
his shirt tail

will stay trimly tucked,
one button will open
at the collar. He will find

some woman who handles
a kerchief well, a woman
who looks good in gloves.

He will give her
a solid reason
to wear black.

Missing Wife

The poster at the truck stop
says she suffers bouts
of amnesia, wanders off,
forgets she is his wife.
The husband is asking around.
Has anyone seen her?
There's a reward, in heavy
black letters, a phone number
and photos of Saturday night
drinking beer on the couch,
and of a wedding, the man
looking sharp in his tuxedo,
the woman in her veil
looking like a tumbleweed
of lace. They are smiling,
cutting the cake. His hand
over hers on the glistening
white knife. This woman

could be anyone. Out there,
walking the street, warming
her face in the afternoon sun,
she is trying new foods
and buying exotic clothes
without the prior knowledge
of her husband. She has not
forgotten how, in the early days
he woke her, doing the soft shoe,
singing, *Good morning, baby,*
how did you sleep?
Nor has she forgotten
the black line of his moustache
hurrying over her, some nights,

as if she were a dark room
he could never find
the switch for. How it came

to his hands around
her throat she does not know.
But she will never forget
her own voice, hoarse,
and no longer her own,
begging him to do it,
do it, to *just fucking
do it*. It was not forgetting

that took this woman.
It was, rather, a rare case
of remembering—remembering
how every day he drew a line
for her, and how she secretly
kept track, by notching the floorboard
where the last line had been.
And after a time she saw
he was cheating her, by fractions
until all that was left
was that immaculate white line
and the blank wall,
against which she posed
for every picture
he took of her.

Finding the Words

When I walk it,
the path to the lost words
will be strewn with socks,
gloves, earrings, all the twins
of things I've lost
on this long journey out.
I'll gather them up like toys
in my skirt, following the thin trail,
this hedge I have kept against
famine, fatigue and loss
of direction. I'll search

for signposts, rings of keys,
all eighteen pairs of sunglasses
ever lost to me. All the fifty-second cards
to the decks I never played, will slip
from my sleeves. Every dead letter
will be returned to me. Along the road,

I'll have a chance to see
my old three dogs named Tippy,
Susie, my one-eyed cat,
all the grandparents,
all the greats and even
my virginity will flush out
from somewhere, pull the last
mauve ribbon from my hair,
as I pass, reeling, now,
in a chariot drawn
by furious stallions,
their crazy manes blazing
a path through the deepest part
of the woods. The forest,

bending to greet us,
leads us to the clearing
where burns the fire that burns
from the center of the earth.

It is here I will dance
my warrior dance, pounding
my feet into the dirt.
I will sit down and sing
this plain song,
long and low and sweet.
Syllables flying
from my tongue
like sparks
from a chip of flint.

A Regular Dervish

True Tribe

don't give me that blood-follows-blood
crap, i want a new tribe. i came through
my mother's water and my father's fire
to get here. my skin may be the color
of newly fallen snow, but i dye my hair
jet black because in art I learned
that a paintbrush dipped many times
in water makes this color. i am not
the unmarked canvas, i am dark water,
and today i'm a black-haired white girl
walking down the street who sees herself
only in the store window's reflection.
i get happy, for instance, when a sioux man
stops me on the sidewalk for a quarter and asks,
what's your tribe. wanting new ancestors,
i say, i'm the daughter of meat-eaters,
who is no longer hungry. this is a lie
(note the leather jacket, shoes, belt).
i learned such duplicity from my grandmother,
of german blood, during world war ii,
who shamed us, shamed us, who
shamed us into america. truthfully,
i'm the daughter of men who scaled
continents to escape learning how
to stand in formation and shoot. farmers
who inhabited land, flat and rolling,
good for planting crops, also good
for waves of advancing troops. hey,
(this is our family boast)
some of the best generals in history
have left our tender roots
trampled in fields.
searching for my true tribe,
i trace the almond shapes
of my eyes, wanting, with the heat
of sex, a hun invader,
knocking down the door
to be my distant grandfather.
not for the victimhood of it, no,

but just to say that something old
and bloody survives in me.
whatever comes to this life,
comes to it through violence.
we live in a country
that dispatches B-2 bombers
if our winter shipment
of kiwi fruit is late.
try to wash the mess
of that, the mess of that,
try to wash
that mess
from your hands.

Getting Ready

i'm the thousand-change girl,
getting ready for school,
standing in my bedroom,
ripping pants and shirts
from my body, trying dresses
and skirts. my father,

at the bottom of the steps
is yelling, the bus
is coming, here comes
the bus. i'm wriggling
into jeans, zippers
grinding their teeth,
buttons refusing
their holes. my brother,

dressed-in-five-minutes,
stands in the hallway,
t-shirt and bookbag
saying, what's the big
problem. i'm kneeling
in front of the closet
foraging for that great-lost-
other-shoe. downstairs,
my father offers advice. slacks,
he's yelling, just put on
some slacks. i'm in the mirror
matching earrings,
nervous fingers
putting the back
to the front. downstairs

the bus is fuming in the yard,
farm kids with cowlicks
sitting in rows. everything's
in a pile on the floor.
after school, mother will scream,
get upstairs and hang up
that mess, but i don't care.

I'm the thousand-change girl,
trotting downstairs now
looking good, looking ready

for school. father, pulling back
from the steps with disgust,
giving me the once over,
saying, is *that*
what you're wearing.

Doing the Twist

Felix has four daughters
just like the Lennon sisters
on the Lawrence Welk television
show. Felix has four daughters,
two altos and two sopranos,
but wouldn't you know,
Felix can't get those girls
to stand together in a straight row,
much less wear the same clothes.
Felix says, I've got four daughters
for all the good it's doing me.
One night, watching the TV, Felix calls
into the kitchen, says, look here girls,
come and see this fellow dancing.
Come and see this crazy
Chubby Checkers. The girls
crowd the doorway, watching
Chubby grind out cigarettes
on the Ed Sullivan show.
One by one, they drop
their shoes. One by one,
they drop their dishtowels,
and in their stocking feet,
they try it, careful at first
on the hardwood floor, doing
the twist. What is going on?
Gladys calls from the kitchen,
doing the dishes by herself.
They're busy, Felix yells,
they're doing the twist.
After this, they do it
for holidays and company
and whenever relatives come
from California. Felix goes
to Bismarck and buys
the record and damn
if those girls can't dance,
twisting in a diamond,
like all the points

on a compass.
The sopranos twisting high,
the altos twisting low,
and the youngest one, they say,
is a regular dervish.

Watching JoAnn Castle Play

Saturday nights, before Mom and Dad
went to polka, we'd watch Lawrence Welk.
We'd watch Bobby throw Cissy and catch her.
Joe Feeney sang *My Wild Irish Rose.*
Arthur Duncan tap danced across the stage.
Lawrence emceeing in that corny German brogue
my father did not hesitate to remind us
he laughed all the way to the bank with.
Everybody singing, everybody swaying
in chiffon and sports coats, everybody smiling
those *that's-entertainment-the-show-*
must-go-on-there's-no-business-like-
show-business smiles. There was one woman
we waited for and that was JoAnn Castle.
JoAnn Castle with her mile-high, honey-blonde
beehive, and her big, big back that never quite fit
into her big backless gowns. Joann Castle
with her hands on the keys, playing
the honky tonk. As we watched from behind
Lawrence counted her off *a one and a two*
and away she would go, her bare arms
flapping her big bottom bouncing,
she'd be jamming the keys, rapping,
like tongues they were flapping.
When she turned to face the camera,
her pearly whites, still tinkling those ivories.
Even the fogeys in the back row felt inclined
to say, JoAnn Castle, man. She's been to Chicago.
She's been to New York. Shit man, I'll bet
she's even been to New Orleans.

The Woman on the Dance

these hips are mighty hips
these hips are magic hips
 —Lucille Clifton

The woman
   the woman
the woman on the dance
                    floor's hips
do not sway or dip or grind.
   They only *swish bump swish bump*
      swish through the songs
      strung together like the beads
on the chain around
her neck.

              The woman on the dance
         floor's hips do not have
         a country, did not vote
for president,
      are scarcely connected
to the arms that rise
   to straighten a hair,
      to the eyes that turn
to study the drummer
   under hot flashing
      lights.

The woman
on the dance floor's hips
   are neutrons
      in an atom,
needing nothing to sustain them,
   nothing to sustain
      them, nothing.

The Attempt

i.
on ludes in the house with the big porch
on second street she tried to o.d. we,
driving by in our van happened to stop.
good thing. we sat, watched her breathe
her goodbyes into the phone. so as not to make
her heart race, we waited for the receiver
to drop. it did. we hauled her *one two*
into the van and drove to the hospital
two blocks away from the house with
the big porch on second street.

ii.
her mother that fluorescent light night,
wringing questions from her kerchief
into the purple seats, turned her knees
to mine, dumb, about the fists full
of ludes, the bags in her drawers,
the man she was doing this all for.

iii.
the next morning, hungry, in her hospital bed,
she asked me how she, last night, looked.
i said i didn't recall, only the medics
running with her, the doors flying open
ahead of us. i did not say, only,
all these years I cannot forget,
her blouse pulled up over her face,
her unsnapped bra, white
and flapping in the wind.

Bronze These Shoes

                    Peter says
I should bronze these platform shoes
that I found in a box marked *keepers*
in my parents' basement. Tan suede
with stars appliqued all around, heels
like paperweights, these shoes

were on my feet the day I went to
my Great Uncle Fred's funeral
and somehow it all comes back to me
when I see them—Fred ranging around
his big messy house in his wheelchair
for he had lost a leg to diabetes, and his wife,

Great Aunt Ida with her one gold tooth
and her cat-eye glasses, who liked to cook
but never liked to do dishes, who had
too many promiscuous daughters,
who stood on the front porch
and waved a hankie when you came

to visit. I wore these shoes
to Fred's funeral, and on that day
I wore a burnt orange minidress
that was all thigh and no hip,
and a heavy streak of eyeliner
and my hair was long and straight
and parted exactly down the middle.

And people took photos of Fred,
I recall, looking cool in his casket.
And all the ladies wept and sweated
in their big flowered dressed. And me,
tromping around, tugging at the hem
of my mini. And Ida, dabbing her eyes

with her hankie. All of us commenting
on how hard it was to believe that Fred

was actually gone. And I think about
those things we leave behind in boxes,
and about Ida who fell flat and died
in a K-Mart ten years later, rushing,
I've always liked to imagine
for some really good blue light special.

My Father Tells This Story about His Brother Frank and the Wick (Every Time I Ask Him for Money)

your grandpa marquart he was a tight sonofabitch, you know, every night he'd come to the bottom of the steps and yell up, frank, go to sleep, you're wasting my oil, because frank liked to read, he was always reading something. he wasn't much for farm work, but he liked school and reading and just wasting his time on books.

so grandpa thought he better put an end to all that laziness and sloth. frank was pretty much worthless when five o'clock chores rolled around. it was more work getting him out of bed than just doing the chores yourself.

so this went on for years, this, grandpa coming to the steps at night and yelling up, frank go to sleep, you're wasting my oil, and frank setting his book down, leaving it open to the last page he was reading and rolling the wick down into the lamp and dousing the flame.

so finally frank gets this town job and makes a little money, and the first thing he does is buys himself some oil right off, see, so he can read as late as he pleases. then when grandpa comes to the steps at night and yells up, frank, go to sleep, you're wasting my oil, frank gets out of bed and goes to the top of the steps and yells back down, this is my oil, I bought this oil with my own money, and I will burn this oil however I see fit.

but grandpa, he had a way, you know, of seeing how things broke down, how they divided up, because he yelled right back, without even thinking, he said, but what about the wick? that's what he said, what about the wick?

your grandfather, i'm telling you, now there was a tight man.

Shit & the Dream of It

All the arts derive from
this ur-act of making.
—W.H. Auden

I was knee-deep in my dad's pole barn,
below zero for two weeks, the milk cows
couldn't go outside. We just spread straw
over the freshest layer and hoped
for warmer weather. I was breaking open
those straw bales spreading them wide
with a pitchfork when I said, hey,
I'm breaking out of this hellhole.
But how far can you get? They say

little kids stand by the toi-toi
and wave bye-bye as the new thing
they made swirls away. It's a stage
they go through. I never went through
stages, I just hopped into whatever
had keys and hauled ass. Listen,

there's no escaping it. Last night
I dreamed I was naked on a commode
in the middle of a room full of high-up
mucky-mucks and they were all
drinking Chablis from some year
better than this one. The stool,
turns out, is an avant garde exhibit
of which I am a working part.
I'm in the center trying to produce
those gems they like, those necessary
nuggets. I cry for paper, a curtain
to wrap around me, but they say, no,

they're interested in process. Process,
I tell them, my ass. You know, my dad
tried to warn me that day I was peeling out
the driveway. Wherever you go, he said,
you'll find it. I don't mean to run on
like this, but he was right. One time,

at a party in the seventies some guy
took a crap on the living room carpet.
Tripping on acid, he mistook himself
for the family dog. He smelled that scent
and went for it. Now, you might want to say

well, that was the times, but listen,
I have plenty of relatives
planted in a hill just north
of my hometown who will tell you
the rotten truth. Everything turns to it.
Just ask the worms. They'll give you
the straightest poop.

Everything's a Verb

boundaries
   or the lack thereof
      the counselor tries to tell me
   are the reason i am in this trouble
        i am in
the counselor wears
   a blunt cut   her blonde fingers delineate
      examples of boundary or lack thereof
   problems
(relationships with younger men
   relationships with older women
      this tendency i have of walking in to
   and out of
      marriages
   some of which were not
      my own) all clear-cut examples
        of boundary or lack thereof
          problems
      i try to explain
   how everything's a verb to me
   the world is an endless array of fibers
weaving and connecting
   unraveling as time passes   time
          itself a construct
         loosely based upon our observations
      of the rate at which the threads go about
   this business of weaving and unraveling
the slower fibers becoming the things
   we name into nouns but they're all verbs
   if one is prepared to take the long view
           boundaries
        the counselor reiterates
        if i could establish clear-cut definitions
      between where i end
   and the rest of the world
        begins   i could put away
      my dragon earrings   retire
   my snake bracelets

cut loose once and for all
my junk yard dog
husband.

The Miracle Baby

She was born with a cunt and a brain.

That's the punchline to a joke told to me.
The question is *Have you heard about*

the miracle baby? and this guy has let me
in on it as if to say, I can tell you're one of those

unflappable broads who doesn't blanche
at the crude, who doesn't feel the whip

on her back, her hide has become so thick.
And I do not disappoint him, I smile

as if I have gotten it, and indeed
I have. Something is flexing in me,

forcing my rib cage wide, my throat
is tightening like a sphincter to contain

this blast that wants to belch out of me
hard like a fist and level everything.

This rage, I'm looking for the spell
to cure it. I'm trying to be the miracle baby,

but I must tell you these days
when I see these men led strictly

to me by their divining rods
something flashes and (I cannot stop

these thoughts) I see them naked
with their little wangers dangling,

and I want to snatch those tender
noodles, for this potion I'm concocting,

for this broth I am brewing,
for this sickness that burns

inside me. The recipe is old,
someone lost it long ago.

I'm making it up, making
it up. I'm forced

to make it up
as I go along.

Knitting

you with the knit-one-purl-two
you with the rosary on the nightstand
shoring up losses, worrying
the beads down to nothing
grandma, bean counter, the world
is unraveling since you left, the cat
got ahold of the skein, he's under
the couch, grandma, deeper
than i know how to go, my arms
are not enough, my arms
cannot reach, my baby
died on a friday, it was clear
the day you left, the cat
got ahold of the skein,
he's under the couch,
grandma, pulling, pulling
pulling those yarns, my arms
are not enough, my arms
cannot reach, my baby
died on a friday, my husband
thinks i'm
                        grandma,
how many stitches in the row
after all that have dropped,
i cannot know, i cannot
know, i cannot know
how to pick them up

The Long Root

The Long Root

Life can only be understood backward,
but it must be lived forward.
—Søren Kierkegaard

i.
She liked to tell jokes.
She told them good, in English,
pausing in the right places
just the way they had been told to her.
But when it came to punchlines,
she leaned toward Grandpa
and said it to him, in German.
The two of them would laugh and rock
in their seats. When I protested
she said, *there's no way to say,*
in English. Some small detour

of meaning, something lost
between the tongue and the brain.
There's no way to say this
in English. On her first trip

to the city she complimented me
on my lack of furniture
and fell upon my waterbed
with the zeal of a woman
who had never been. I left her there
to test it, returning to find her
grounded out on the sideboard—
her legs too short to reach
the floor, her bottom lodged

in the crack and too wide
to do anything about.

Help me out the bed, she said.
And we joined hands—me,
planting a foot and tugging;
she, rocking in the crevice,
until we laughed her loose.

                Tonight
she is a horizontal ruin,
a mountain of secrets.
I have driven the deep funnel
of night, walked the endless
fluorescence of corridors
to witness this, her final trip
to the city. Her heartbeat
cuts a ragged path
on the glowing screen
above. She breathes
when the machine says so.
The nurses are familiar
with her body, rolling her over
saying, *Lydia, you bad girl,*
you have been throwing off
your covers again.

I am in the corner,
quiet as Lydia.
The nurses do not tell me
how sometimes the hearing
is the last to go.

ii.

I always wanted stories of the place
where she had come from.
I wanted stale bread
shared between many hands
and stony fields passed through
in the middle of the night.
I wanted superstitious women
dancing around campfires,
but when I asked she said,
you can't get there from here.
Some small detour of meaning,
something lost between the tongue
and the brain. Never long

on description, even less so now.
Lydia, bad girl, Black Sea German,
with a history of reinventing
the language. Secrets
were her craft, misinformation

her trade. When I got to the first grade
and found out somersaults
were not called *butzle books*,
I was not bitter. And later
when I discovered lovers
did not appreciate being called
poopsie pie, I tried to stop
but every time I went to pinch them
this is what came out.

                    She imagined
all these years that I was Little Debbie
of breakfast food fame. Every letter
she sent contained a picture of me
carved off a donut box, her knife
having rounded precisely,
each fine feature,
each luxurious curl.

      Little Debbie,
that consummate image
of sweetness taped to the top
of her letter. Underneath, her words
all running together about thunderstorms
and ministers and tomatoes coming ripe,
words about cataracts fogging her vision,
and missing me. Inside the envelope

folded many times like secret missives
were fashion ads torn from
glamour magazines. In them
models with glossy hair,
rush into city streets
hailing taxis. Always
they are smiling,
always they are raising
their thin arms
in the air.

iii.

I stood vigil over her
the day Grandfather died.
She was a wreck
in a cotton nightgown.
Her queen-size bed supported her
wracking side to side like a child
with a high fever. She walked in
while they tried to resuscitate
him. She saw a circle of uniforms,
a nurse forced her from the room,
they lost him anyway,
she never had a chance
to say goodbye. I remember

the day he pulled a rotten molar
from his mouth with a pliers,
the smug look on his face
when he came to the kitchen
to show us the long root.
He said, *I brought this tooth
with me from Odessa.*
                              Odessa
Black Sea city of lost
and forgotten memories,
no matter how I stretch
my craft, I still cannot
find your shores. I recall

the long root of a wart
digging deeper into my hand,
each day she worried over it.
Wart sounding like *war*
when she told me the word.
For years, I thought I'd had a war
on my hand. Down the street,

she dragged me to the *brauchere*,
an old healer who yodeled,
from her widow's walk
each morning. The *brauchere* tied

233

a string to my finger, bent over,
crooned to my wormy wound.
Coins were exchanged, the string
was buried outside. Afterward

for my troubles, I got a taste
of Grandpa's rhubarb wine.
The same wine that knocked me
on my ass every time I came over
for Sunday dinner. In those days,

Grandpa made the rounds with his tray
of shot glasses. *One glass*
for everybody, no matter
how small. After dinner
we did tipsy dishes. Grandma
washed, Grandpa dried, I
would put away.

iv.

The last time
I saw Lydia
she was standing
in her kitchen, squat
on her feet like a sugar bowl
in an apron, making sauerkraut—
chopped cabbage heads, ripe
and rank, boiling in kettles
on her stove. *He likes it*,
she said, nodding at Gotthelf,
her stroke-struck second husband.
He was hanging on the ledge
of his chair, smiling
his eye teeth out.

V.

That card game
we used to play, *duruch*,
which I never knew the meaning of
or understood how to play,
but somehow always in the end,
things came around for me. A deuce
took on rare significance,
a red card was considered good.
She would poke me, say the cards
seemed to like me, tell me
I had luck. I always knew
she was lying. Years later

a student of Russian told me *duruch*
means *you fool.* Odessa,
you long cold country,
you were nothing more
than her point of departure.
I was the country
she came to. It's time

to take the wringer washer
out of her basement
and dismantle it, time to untie
the hot towels she wrapped
around my head to relieve
the migraines I inherited
from her. It's time to loosen

their grip. And that old *brauchere*
she took me to who cured me
of ringworm by saying a prayer
and burying a lock
of my hair, it's time
to let her go too. I must

dig up what was buried
and repeat the words
she said. I must
say them to myself.
I must say them
backward.

This Room Full of Nothing

Weaver

Woman of thread
    woman of silks and yarns
come to the city
    where your dark-hearted sister
        lies in wait
like pest-under-stone
    for a whiff
        for a movement of you

Come to the hair rising
    on the back of the neck
        to the fierce pulsing in arms
Oh weaver woman
    woman of saved string   come
        to the city and see
this vain lump
    I have grown up
        from silence

Come then come
    and we shall unravel
        and weave them well
the many strands of stories
    grown tangled   grown
        convoluted within.

Gravity's First Lesson

tired of raging, i've decided
to go gently. remember that
balloon game we played
as kids, *keep it up, keep*
it up, don't let it touch
the ground. always one kid
willing to grate his cheddar knees
on the carpet. oh, i was good

at that. remember dodge ball.
ten kids in a circle winging
balls at the ones in the middle,
how they always aimed for
the sweet spots—the head
the crotch, the tender budding
breasts. oh, i was the master
dodger. i had a side-step,
a head-fake, a tremendous
high splits jump. oh, no one

could put me out. remember tag,
how we ran with terror from
the one who was it, threw our bodies
down spider-webbed crags,
held our breath behind
heart-pounding corners,
hiding from the one who carried
that terrible transforming touch
on his fingertips. oh, i was never it,
never it, i never wanted

to be it. once, at a rock concert
i saw 50,000 fans moan and heave
to keep a beachball in the air.
50,000 roaring bodies agreeing
with the precision of marines
on this one thing, *we must*
keep it up, keep it up,
never let it touch
the ground. so,

the earth wants me. is this
gravity's first lesson. tired
of raging, i've decided to
let myself go
gently.

Gatherings

Having let the people of our youth
slip away, we come to these rooms
filled with those from the youths

of others. And you are with the woman
in sequins, and I am with the younger man,
and tonight we ride the conversation

like old sea captains dodging the iceberg
that was our marriage. But I remember
weekday mornings in 1982, your blue Chevy

worn old and silver from the sun, floating
into my alley. You, slamming the screen door
to gather me. Inside, your hands lifted

books from my shelves, hoping only
to trace the words my eyes had seen.
Watching you lift and turn trinkets

in the air, I imagined your touch,
so gentle and full of awe, would always read
my finer lines. Oh, the tricks

some hands can play. Tonight,
I see that touch, soft like a reminder
on her waist, sequins glimmering

in the light, as simply the touch
one stranger reserves
for another, and I know

that when this night is over
we will drift away, caught up
in the streams of others,

drifting and drifting, ceasing
finally to flow to these rooms
where we will find each other.

Losing track eventually
of the comings, of the goings
of the other.

History of a Portrait

Somewhere she has lost her glass
and all that holds her now is a thin frame.
The woman on the wall is veiled in white

that shows its shadows in blue and gray.
Her dress swirls, blown by breezes
from another canvas. A gift from a man

who loved the sight of a face
he could never see, the canvas
still bears traces of a barbeque,

ground into her one mad night
by another man who popped
each egg in the refrigerator

and shredded the houseplants
over the yellow carpet. She is not
dancing. She is shielding herself

from the wind. Scratched, wrinkled
and viewed too many times,
she continues to appear

over the bed, over the couch,
over the kitchen table.
Never once raising her eyes

to see who it is that is going
and who is coming next
in her direction.

Riding Shotgun Through Iowa With Quest

this musician's life.
play until one,
pack up, get paid.
send the dancers
home drunk, sweaty,
clinging to each other.
on the long way home
I ride shotgun with Quest
helping keep watch
over the night. our talk
turns to women and
death, what Quest calls
all things inevitable.
he is not so afraid
of the final embrace
as the moment before,
the arms stretched out
to us, the looking into
the eyes of it. in the dead
of this night, we agree
to trust it, the good faith
of this road running
beneath us. I tell him how
this place is like my home,
where every night
vapor lights burn
in yards, and every morning
farmers rise at dawn to milk
the cows. not for me
that life. in a family
of settlers, I was
the immigrant.
fixing my eye
on the horizon,
setting myself to reel
madly across
this continent. flying
through Iowa, past
cornfields and silos,

the two-storied houses
our dancers have gone
to sleep in, I doze,
wake, doze, to find Quest
hands on the wheel
trying to outdistance
the road. five a.m.
passing a farmyard
I see my father step out
to do the morning chores.
his shadow, bending
to pet the dog becomes
my brother. this is the time
of accidents, the ones
we'll never see.
we pass through
knowing that soon
the sun will show
it's awful face, that soon
even our headlights
will be worthless.

Acts of Preservation

—*for Thea Kati*

i.   Every story she tells
ends with someone dying. From the tip
of her left hand to the tip of her right,
span the yarns of the six generations
she's known. Births. Lives. Deaths.
She pulls them all around, one on top
of the other, until they are knit tightly
together. The easy chair is right where
he left it. On the first night, we are careful
not to sit there, after she says, *No man*
to this earth, will ever take his place.
Out of plastic she brings a scarf he gave her,
the gold silk faded to a soft yellow.
Thirty bucks, she says, this would cost today.

ii.   It has been twenty years
since he left her alone in this cold country
to which he brought her, a seventeen-year-old
bride. It was her sister he was really after,
the most beautiful girl in the village.
The way she tells it, he waited too long
to return home, by the time he got there,
the sister was married. But she reminded him
enough of her sister, so he proposed,
via letter to her father, who replied,
you need to ask my daughter
face-to-face. Maybe you don't like her.
Maybe she don't like you. This was 1925.
Erikousa, Greece. She still loves her father
for this.

iii.   And on the last night,
she takes us to her bedroom, throws open
her bureau to the many white shirts cradled
in tissue, some wrapped in the original plastic,
all the price tags say $2.75. *Never worn,*
she keeps repeating, *never been worn.*
She asks Peter to try one and it fits.
She twirls him around to face the mirror,
runs her old hands down his back.
Such wide shoulders, she says, rolling
the sleeves up to his elbows. And this
 is how we spend our last night,
watching Peter try on twenty-five
dress shirts. Even though
they are all white. Even though
she cannot read English, we still know,
they are all the same size.

The Crossing

A little twig in green shuffled her tennies
the corner of 10th and 12th this morning.

Impatient for fluorescent orange crossing guards,
she shifted side to side stomping her feet.

There was a general rush of traffic, workers,
late for work, trying to wrench distance

from each second. I had a left on green.
It was my turn. Cars collected behind me.

She started off the curb, then jumped back,
her face cast down to the concrete,

all her safety lessons unlearned.
I signaled her safe and she bolted,

little legs like tiny gears motoring
the distance of a crossing.

She made small progress
through car grilles and paint striping.

Mounting the curb on the other side,
she ambled down the sidewalk,

her body swinging loosely to school.
I would have turned immediately,

to recover the distance I had lost,
but I noticed, idling in the lane

next to me, a couple with glasses,
mid-fifties, stopped on the green,

both heads turned far
down the sidewalk. The man

kept his hands on the wheel.
The woman looked like

she was about to say something.

Small Town Cafe

Tonight while the men
have gone home to their wives
and the teenagers to their cars,
only the three old bachelors
full of coffee and gossip,
sit by the window and watch
as traffic rolls by. The cook

in greasy glasses, has emerged
from the cave of the kitchen,
with a yellow fly swatter
in her hand, bent to kill
all winged intruders.
I follow in white shoes
wiping the splattered tables
with this wet rag. The owner

smokes and watches from behind
the counter. She has designer
eyeglasses and fingernails
and a limp that even her mink
won't let you forget. Coffee
is ten cents, but if a strange car
pulls up, full of new suits
with briefcases, she will lift
herself from the stool, limp
across the room and whisper,
charge them twenty-five.

Grandfather's Hands

Grandfather's hands in the sausage tub,
where I sat for hours and watched him

add salt, pepper, garlic, salt, pepper,
garlic, then knead everything together

with his hairy knuckles. His hairy knuckles
reminding me of Brezhnev's eyebrows

on the steering wheel, driving me
to school in the fan-tailed Chevy

at five miles an hour. Left turns
taking an eternity of stutter steps

inch-by-inch, not hand-over-hand
like my brother was learning

in Driver's Ed. Grandfather's hands
on the wheel, Memorial Day drives

to Tappen, to put flowers
on the boys' graves. The two

small wreaths riding with me
in the back seat like well-behaved

children. The silence in the car
afterward, except for the sound

of the blinker from the last left turn,
clicking on and off all the way home.

Riding Back to Town

Just as he came from water,
so he returned to it.
His preoccupation,
the final years, was fishing.
Every day he'd load
his tackle box and drive
thirty miles to the nearest lake,
coming home at sundown
with nothing, as far as I
ever saw. I went with him once.
Riding home in silence
I felt good. In the presence
of his siren sisters-in-law,
he could sit for hours, hands
folded over his stomach.
To all questions he gave
answers without handles.
We wandered off, replies
clutched under arms
like immigrants with poor
luggage. He is gone,
a long time now. Strange
how this thirty miles
reminds me of him.
In the distance
a stream of water
moves across
a field of stones.
I get the feeling
I'm riding back to town
with no fish.

Resurrection

A rose by your bedside you would never know,
the nurses tried to tell me. I tried to tell them

how you always knew to plant the tulips
beside the dahlias, inside the ring of gladioli

and leave a space in the middle,
the place I always found you

when I came to visit. Hard to believe,
you are gone, almost two years now

and this lily, given to me
last Easter to help me through

the first year, how I swore
I'd keep it alive all year.

You would have laughed at my despair
when it began to make its slow descent

back to the earth. First the white trumpets
dropping off, then leaf after leaf retracting

until all that was left was the brown stalk
which I cut down to nothing. It disgusted

me so. *Alone, through a valley, we all
must walk*, an old man told me

at your funeral. You would have laughed
at my surprise when the green shoots

appeared. *Weeds*, I thought
but watered them, and now they are lilies

three of them, climbing back out
of themselves, preparing to tell it

all over again. These things we call miracles.
It would be enough to make you laugh.

The Blizzard Rope

I have not forgotten,
ten and still holding
the blizzard rope you tied
around my waist, winter
of sixty-six. You said,
you are home base,
and stepped out
into weather. Snow

like a house built
around us. Holsteins
holding their milk
in the hungry barn.
You had no choice.
The straight path
you walked every day
a mystery, in this weather.
I have not forgotten,
thirty-three and holding
the blizzard rope.

White-out, you step out.
Your fine hands
climbing weather,
your dark coat, lost
to the great white.
Your footsteps
filling now with
weather. The line
has grown icy, Father.
The weather worsens.
I am home base.
Go where you will.

Somewhere in a House Where You Are Not

There is sunlight coming through windows
somewhere in a house where you are not.

An old man and old woman eating breakfast
to the sound of the clock, out of words,

empty of thoughts, but for who died this year
and of what. If you follow the sun to that house

you will find the long lost driveway
that no highway intersects, the loose gravel

crackling under your wheels, the sun breaking
cleanly free of a horizon. You must park.

You must come to an absolute halt
outside the house where you are not,

letting your many necessary miles drop
from your bones like dust. Sit and wait.

Do not fear the mop-faced dog. He pounds
his tail for you. He is uninterested

in your tires. The old woman will soon come,
peeking through the ancient blinds, saying,

who on earth, and seeing your face
will hold out her hands, warm and soft

as good black dirt, and take you inside,
the house filling with your arrival,

the old man smiling his surprised skeleton smile,
the old woman asking, have you come far,

was it a long drive, are you hungry, are you
tired, to which you may answer, yes

and lie down in the bed they have kept
empty in your absence, reserved for the day

you would need this room full of nothing,
but rare morning light, and the stroke

of an old brown hand, inviting you
to rest, to sleep, to feel the earth

revolve slowly around and around
without you.

Acknowledgments

Many thanks to the editors and advocates who have labored so patiently over the books contained in this manuscript: Bill Truesdale (*Everything's a Verb*); Marilyn Johnson and Dorianne Laux (*From Sweetness*); Suzzanne Kelley and Thom Tammaro (*Small Buried Things*); and Suzzanne Kelley and Nayt Rundquist, who were instrumental in bringing *Gratitude with Dogs under Stars* into the world. Deepest gratitude to you all. Many thanks to the arts editors, book teams, and publishing interns at New Rivers Press (Minnesota State University Moorhead) and North Dakota State University Press, who worked on the books contained in this New & Collected volume.

Thanks to the Pearl Hogrefe Foundation at Iowa State University, the Ragdale Foundation, the Ucross Foundation, the Iowa Arts Council, the Virginia Center for the Creative Arts, and Humanities Iowa for grants and fellowships which enabled the early work to be completed.

I'm grateful to the National Endowment for the Arts for an NEA Fellowship and the College of Liberal Arts & Sciences at Iowa State University for an LAS Faculty Fellowship and sabbaticals that supported the completion of this research, and thanks to the Academy of American Poets for a Poets Laureate Fellowship that supported my work as Poet Laureate of the state of Iowa.

I also wish to thank Brenna Gerhardt and the staff at Humanities North Dakota for grants that enabled me to complete this work. Thanks to the Arcus Center for Social Justice Leadership at Kalamazoo College for a Social Justice Fellowship in the Spring of 2015.

A special thanks to Dr. Roger Hanson, an alumnus of Iowa State University, who established the Roger S. Hanson Faculty Support Fund in Creative Writing. As the inaugural recipient of this gift, I am forever grateful to Dr. Hanson for his support of my work.

Writers would not survive without friends, and I'm grateful to so many fellow artists (some now gone, some still here) who have sustained me through critical times: Barbara Crow, Glenna Henderson, Sheryl St. Germain, Ted Kooser, Stephen Pett, Mary Swander, David Zimmerman, Charissa Menefee, Kenny Cook, Ned Balbo, Jane Satterfield, Jon Billman, Benjamin Percy, Romeo Oriogun, Peter Maneisis, Anthony Stevens,

Adrianne Kalfopoulou, Indigo, Moor, Suzanne Strempek Shea, Michael Kimball, Jenny O'Connell, Elizabeth Searle, Justin Tussing, Robin Talbot, Rick Bass, Ingrid Lilligren, Michael Miller, and Charles Kostelnick. I'm also grateful to mentors who were associated with MSUM when I was a young developing writer in the 1980s—Sally Herrin, Richard Zinober, Alan R. Davis, Thom Tammaro, David Mason, Richard DuBord, and Mark Vinz. May we all have the good fortune to be surrounded by a nurturing and inspiring community at the start of our writing lives.

Finally, I wish to thank my many colleagues in the MFA Program in Creative Writing and Environment at Iowa State University and the Stonecoast Low-Residency MFA Program at University of Southern Maine—who are far too numerous to mention, but whose influence and inspiration have kept me going as a writer all these years. Deepest gratitude.

I'm grateful to my family, especially my parents Gladys and Felix Marquart and my siblings, Colleen, Charlotte, Richard, and Judy, who stuck with me over the years. Lastly, I'm grateful to my partner, Thomas Rice, and for his sons, Adam Rice and Gabe Rice, who have taken me in as family and made life more interesting and worthwhile. All my love.

| Everything's a Verb

Charlotte Poetry Review, *Circumference*, *Cumberland Poetry Review*, *Half Tones to Jubilee*, *Loonfeather*, *Poet Lore*, *Southern Poetry Review*, *Zone 3*, *Clearing Space Anthology* (Wordshop, Ltd., 1993), *A Circle of Four* (Dacotah Territory Press, 1989)

| From Sweetness

Connecticut Review, *Cumberland Poetry Review*, *Half Tones to Jubilee*, *Kalliope*, *Many Mountains Moving*, *Mississippi Review*, *North American Review*, *Passages North*, *Red Weather*, *River City*, *South Dakota Review*, *Southern Poetry Review*, *Spoon River Anthology*, *Threepenny Review*, *Witness*, *The Talking of Hands: New Rivers 30th Anniversary Anthology* (New Rivers Press, 1998), *The Hunger Bone: Rock & Roll Stories* (New Rivers Press, 2001)

"Palimpsest" was commissioned by the Iowa State University Museums to accompany a public art project, Doug Shelton's mural, *Unlimited Possibilities*, 1997.

| Small Buried Things

Brevity, Comstock Review, Georgetown Review, The Ledge, Mississippi Review, Narrative Magazine, The Normal School, North American Review, Oberon Review, Opium, Rattle, River Styx, RUNES: A Review of Poetry, Southern Poetry Review

| New Poems

Stone Gathering: A Reader, Terrain.org: A Journal of Built + Natural Environments, North American Review, Des Moines Register, Steve Kowit Prize, San Diego Poetry Annual, 30 Days Hath September, Poems for the Moment, Prairie Public Radio, Grist: A Journal of Literary Arts

"Come November" was reprinted in *Dear America: Letters of Hope, Habitat, Defiance, and Democracy*, edited by Simmons Buntin, Elizabeth Dodd, and Derek Sheffield, Trinity University Press, 2020.

Notes | "Small Buried Things"

The long poem, "Small Buried Things," draws details from articles and news reports about North Dakota's oil boom. Below is a listing of the articles and media sources that were consulted in the writing of the poem.

"Air Force: N.D. Oil Drilling Poses No Threat to Underground Nuclear Missiles." *Twincities.com*, posted April 12, 2012, http://www.twincities.com/ci_20384362/air-force-n-d-oil-drilling-poses-no.

Battistoni, Alyssa. "Does Fracking Cause Earthquakes?" *Blue Marble: Mother Jones*, posted April 16, 2012, http://www.motherjones.com/blue-marble/2012/04/does-fracking-cause-earthquakes.

Behar, Michael. "Whose Fault?" *Mother Jones*, March/April 2013, 32–64.

Dobb, Edwin. "The New Oil Landscape." *National Geographic*, March 2013, 26–59.

Donovan, Lauren. "Helms says EPA Could Halt Fracking in Oil Patch." *Bismarck Tribune*, posted November 27, 2011, http://bismarcktribune.com/news/state-and-regional/helms-says-epa-could-halt-fracking-in-oil-patch/article_fe9a3284-18b9-11e1-ba39-001cc4c03286.html.

Fox, Josh, dir. *Gasland*. Documentary, 2010, DVD.

Fox, Josh, dir. *Gasland II*. Documentary, 2013, DVD.

Hutton, Noah, dir. *Crude Independence*. Documentary, 2009, DVD.

Jervin, Sara. "The Fracking Frenzy's Impact on Women." The Center for Media and Democracy's PR Watch, posted April 4, 2012, http://www.prwatch.org/news/2012/04/11204/fracking-frenzys-impact-women.

Johnson, Robert. "Strippers Can Earn $350,000 A Year In This Oil Boomtown Club." *Business Insider*, posted January 17, 2013, http://www.businessinsider.com/williston-north-dakota-oil-boomtown-high-paying-stripper-demand-2013-1?op=1.

Manning, Richard. "Bakken Business: The Price of North Dakota's Fracking Boom." *Harper's Magazine*, March 2013, 29–37.

Niman, Michael. "6 Scary Extreme Energy Sources Being Tapped to Fuel the Post Peak Oil Economy." Seemorerocks Blog: Dirty Energy in the Post Peak Oil World, posted April 15, 2012, http://www.alternet.org/story/154936/6_scary_extreme_energy_sources_being_tapped_to_fuel_the_post_peak_oil_economy (site discontinued).

Shepard, Susan Elizabeth. "Wildcatting: A Stripper's Guide to the Modern American Boomtown." *Buzzfeed*, posted July 13, 2013, http://www.buzzfeed.com/susanelizabethshepardwildcatting-a-strippers-guide-to-the-modern-american-boomtow (site discontinued).

Smith, Matt and Thom Patterson. "Debate over Fracking, Quakes Get Louder." CNN U.S., updated June 15, 2012, http://www.cnn.com/2012/06/15/us/fracking-earthquakes/index.html.

Switchboard: North Dakota Resources Defense Council Staff Blog. "A Suspected Cause of Drinking Water Contamination." Posted December 19, 2011, http://switchboard.nrdc.org/blogs/amall/incidents_where_hydraulic_frac.html (site discontinued).

Walsh, Bryan. "The Truth About Oil." *Time*, April 9, 2012, 29–35.

About | Debra Marquart

Debra Marquart is a Distinguished Professor of Liberal Arts & Sciences and teaches in the MFA Program in Creative Writing and Environment at Iowa State University, as well as the Stonecoast Low-Residency MFA Program at University of Southern Maine. Marquart serves as Iowa's Poet Laureate and the Senior Editor of *Flyway: Journal of Writing & Environment*. The author of seven books—including *The Horizontal World: Growing Up Wild in the Middle of Nowhere* and *Small Buried Things: Poems*—Marquart has been featured on NPR and the BBC and has received over 50 grants and awards including an NEA Fellowship, a PEN USA Award, a *New York Times* Editors' Choice award, and *Elle Magazine*'s Elle Lettres Award.

A singer-songwriter and former road musician, Marquart is a member of The Bone People, a jazz-poetry, rhythm & blues project, with whom she has recorded two CDs—*A Regular Dervish* and *Orange Parade*. She continues to perform live with The Bone People and as a solo artist. In 2021, Marquart was awarded a Poets Laureate Fellowship from the Academy of American Poets. Her most recent books are *The Night We Landed on the Moon: Essays Between Exile & Belonging* (2021) and a poetry collection, *Gratitude with Dogs under Stars: New & Collected Poems* (2023). For more information: debramarquart.com

About | NDSU Press

North Dakota State University Press (NDSU Press) exists to stimulate and coordinate interdisciplinary regional scholarship. These regions include the Red River Valley, the state of North Dakota, the plains of North America (comprising both the Great Plains of the United States and the prairies of Canada), and comparable regions of other continents. We publish peer reviewed regional scholarship shaped by national and international events and comparative studies.

Neither topic nor discipline limits the scope of NDSU Press publications. We consider manuscripts in any field of learning. We define our scope, however, by a regional focus in accord with the press's mission. Generally, works published by NDSU Press address regional life directly, as the subject of study. Such works contribute to scholalry knowledge of region (that is, discovery of new knowledge) or to public consciousness of region (that is, dissemination of information, or interpretation of regional experience). Where regions abroad are treated, either for comparison or because of ties to those North American regions of primary concern to the press, the linkages are made plain. For nearly three-quarters of a century, NDSU Press has published substantial trade books, but the line of publications is not limited to that genre. We also publish textbooks (at any level), reference books, anthologies, reprints, papers, proceedings, and monographs. The press also considers works of poetry or fiction, provided they are established regional classics or they promise to assume landmark or reference status for the region. We select biographical or autobiographical works carefully for their prospective contribution to regional knowledge and culture. All publications, in whatever genre, are of such quality and substance as to embellish the imprint of NDSU Press.

We changed our imprint to North Dakota State University Press in January 2016. Prior to that, and since 1950, we published as the North Dakota Institute for Regional Studies Press. We continue to operate under the umbrella of the North Dakota Institute for Regional Studies, located at North Dakota State University.